*Hotfooting it across searing pavement in South Africa's Kruger National Park,
a flap-necked chameleon ferries a hitchhiking grasshopper.*

Animal Kingdoms

Wildlife Sanctuaries of the World

Prepared by the Book Division
National Geographic Society, Washington, D.C.

$\mathcal{R}$eadjusting to the wild, a once captive female orangutan samples freedom at Camp Leakey, in Tanjung Puting National Park of Indonesian Borneo. Run by primatologist Biruté Galdikas, the camp serves both as research site and rehab center, where orphaned animals and former pets learn to fend for themselves until they can reenter the natural world. PRECEDING PAGES: Emperor penguins crowd Cape Roget, on the edge of the world's largest and coldest wildlife sanctuary: Antarctica.

Animal Kingdoms
Wildlife Sanctuaries of the World

Contributing Authors: Patrick R. Booz,
Douglas Botting, Kenneth Brower, Tom
Melham, Graham Pizzey, Anthony Smith

Published by The National Geographic Society
Gilbert M. Grosvenor,
President and Chairman of the Board
Michela A. English, *Senior Vice President*

Prepared by The Book Division
William R. Gray, *Vice President and Director*
Charles Kogod, *Assistant Director*
Barbara A. Payne, *Editorial Director*

Staff for this book
Barbara A. Payne, *Project Editor*
Toni Eugene, *Text Editor*
Tom Melham, *Assistant Text Editor*
David Ross, *Illustrations Editor*
Suez B. Kehl, *Art Director*
Ann N. Kelsall, Anne E. Withers, *Researchers*
Richard M. Crum, Seymour L. Fishbein,
Ron Fisher, Tom Melham, Jennifer C. Urquhart,
Picture Legend Writers
Carolinda E. Hill, *Contributing Editor*
Carl Mehler, *Map Editor*
Joseph F. Ochlak, *Map Researcher*
James Huckenpahler, *Map Production*
Richard S. Wain, *Production Project Manager*
Lewis R. Bassford, *Production*
Karen Dufort Sligh, *Illustrations Assistant*
Sandra F. Lotterman, *Editorial Assistant*
Karen F. Edwards, Elizabeth G. Jevons,
Peggy J. Oxford, *Staff Assistants*

Manufacturing and Quality Management
George V. White, *Director*
John T. Dunn, *Associate Director*
Vincent P. Ryan, *Manager*
R. Gary Colbert, *Executive Assistant*

Elisabeth MacRae-Bobynskyj, *Indexer*

Library of Congress CIP Data: page 200

*FOLLOWING PAGES: Gemsboks, a type
of antelope characterized by long, swordlike
horns, punctuate the stark and angular
realm of Namib-Naukluft Park in Africa.*

Introduction
by Tom Melham

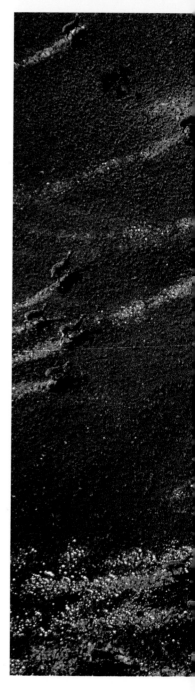

One of countless Hollywood scenes deeply etched upon my brain—no doubt the result of a childhood spent watching too many old movies—concerns *The Hunchback of Notre Dame*. It's the part where the young and heavily made-up Charles Laughton (in the title role) rescues the heroine, then scales the cathedral with her to rasp out gleefully from its heights, "Sanctuary! Sanctuary!"

Among other things, that memorable and emotion-filled scene reminds me that the concept of setting aside sanctuaries for wildlife is very new. It would have struck all but our most recent ancestors as ironic, even unintelligible. For most of time, wild animals ran rampant amid the vast wildernesses that dominated the world; "sanctuaries" were safe spots for *people*. Today, of course, the situation is totally reversed: Mankind runs wild, while nature hews more and more to isolated islands of wildness we call wildlife sanctuaries. But what makes a sanctuary?

Surely national parks and game reserves such as exist in Botswana's antelope-rich Okavango Delta (right) qualify, since they generally ban harrassment and killing of animals. America's wildlife refuges also fit the bill, for although they permit hunting, that hunting is regulated. But what of national forests and other federal tracts, open not only to hunting but also to logging, ranching, mining, and other pursuits often at odds with wildlife? What about wild areas that lack any governmental protection, such as private lands or regions that remain undeveloped simply because they lie too far from current population centers—are *they* wildlife sanctuaries?

To the writers and editors of this book the answer is a resounding *Yes*. Even officially sanctioned reserves are not immune from poaching or poor enforcement, nor from less obvious but even more damaging human activities such as draining wetlands or depleting the ozone layer. Any refuge exists only as long as human society—not mere law—allows it to exist. So it is that this book defines "sanctuaries" in the broadest sense: Places where wildlife enjoys some measure of protection, whether or not that protection stems from governmental decree or something as ephemeral as physical remoteness. Thus a logged forest, a private estate—even a cattle ranch—can serve also as a wildlife refuge, if its ecological makeup helps wildlife

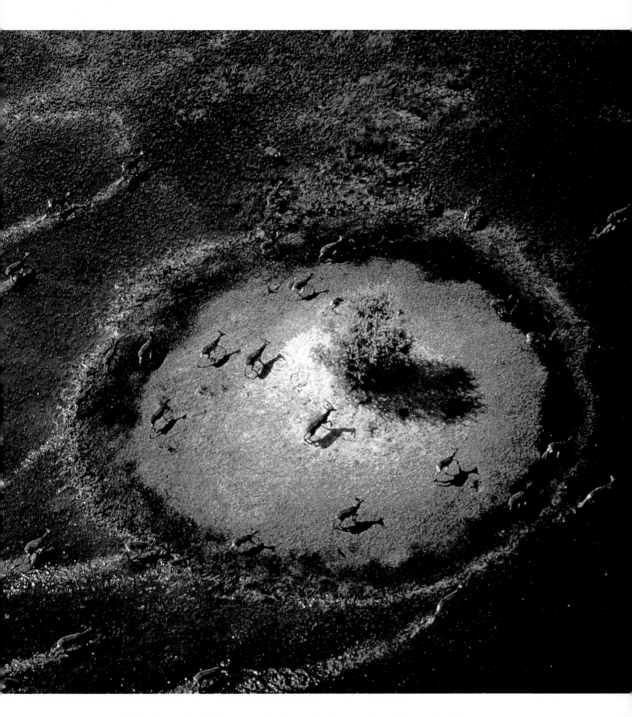

survive. The Danube Delta may be heavily farmed and despoiled by pollution, yet even it remains pivotal for many wild species, especially birds.

All together, the world's official and de facto wildlife reserves number in the tens of thousands. Obviously, any book on this topic can be but a sampler. Yet that is as it should be. Wildlife is not some sanitized collection to be trotted out for display, on demand—not even in today's thoroughly globalized village. Being wild, wild animals occur wherever you find them; so, too, do the world's wildlife sanctuaries.

Africa

High grasses tempt a plains zebra in the savanna of Kenya in East Africa.
Remarkably diverse animal life survives on the second largest continent.

*T*HE ANTELOPE BOUNDED along beside me. It could have departed speedily on its long legs, but chose to keep me company. I was on a motorbike, roughly midway between Cape Town and Cairo, and this splendid creature was the first animal to grant me the honor of such communion. Except for monkeys scampering across the road ahead and one extremely distant elephant, the antelope was the first sizable mammal I had seen in more than 2,000 miles of travel through a continent allegedly bursting with wildlife. The beautiful animal, galloping in parallel, whetted my appetite for seeing others. Its hide had a luster unseen in any zoo. Its legs seemed too slender for the task they were performing. Its tiny hoofs created no more than puffs of dust with every stride. I was enchanted, and then miserable when a bridge loomed, forcing—as I expected—my partner to go elsewhere.

No wonder that at the very next community of humans I asked where animals might be seen in greater numbers. Thus it happened that I

Cabbage-shaped groundsels dot the slopes of Mount Kenya National Park's cloud-kissed peaks. A hippopotamus bursts from waters in the Okavango Delta. Across Africa's vast expanses of savanna, forest, and desert ranges the world's most extensive array of large mammals.

Africa

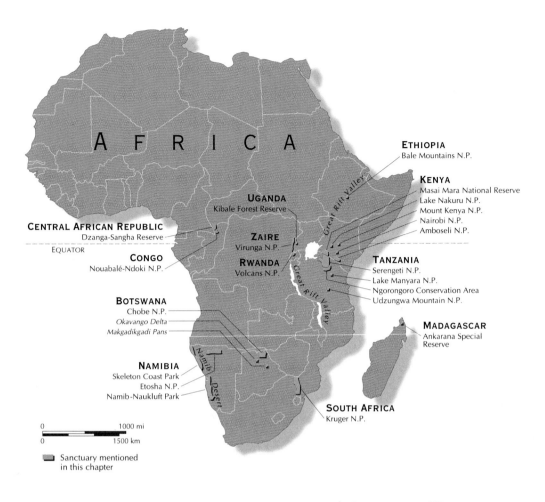

ETHIOPIA
Bale Mountains N.P.

KENYA
Masai Mara National Reserve
Lake Nakuru N.P.
Mount Kenya N.P.
Nairobi N.P.
Amboseli N.P.

CENTRAL AFRICAN REPUBLIC
Dzanga-Sangha Reserve

EQUATOR

CONGO
Nouabalé-Ndoki N.P.

UGANDA
Kibale Forest Reserve

ZAIRE
Virunga N.P.

RWANDA
Volcans N.P.

TANZANIA
Serengeti N.P.
Lake Manyara N.P.
Ngorongoro Conservation Area
Udzungwa Mountain N.P.

BOTSWANA
Chobe N.P.
Okavango Delta
Makgadikgadi Pans

MADAGASCAR
Ankarana Special
Reserve

NAMIBIA
Skeleton Coast Park
Etosha N.P.
Namib-Naukluft Park

SOUTH AFRICA
Kruger N.P.

0   1000 mi
0   1500 km

Sanctuary mentioned
in this chapter

first heard the names Manyara, Serengeti, and Ngorongoro. "For animals," advised my informants, "you have to visit a reserve." One solid preconception about the continent in which I had spent so little time crumbled. Would I never meet herds as I traveled the Great North Road (happy title for a thin ribbon of track from south to north that sometimes failed entirely)? Would single roadside antelopes have to serve in place of myriad nature—on the hoof, the paw, the foot—in all its forms?

"Yes, you must visit a park," said the group, "but you will not be permitted to do so."

"And why not?" I asked sharply, still ignorant of a whole continent's enthusiasm for giving the good news before tacking on the bad.

"Vehicles with only two wheels are forbidden," my advisors asserted, as their children added up my wheels—many more times than once—and always found just two. Hiring four wheels was out of the question. In those student days, I could ill afford paying to share a ride in someone's car, or even coming up with park entrance fees.

"So what are they like, these parks?" I asked the group, as I stood astride my bike in the northern part of what was then Tanganyika.

"We, too, are ignorant of them," came the joint reply. "They are

Africa

not for us. They are for visitors. They are for people with four wheels who come to see what we can see no more."

It was 1955. I was traveling right through the continent possessing the greatest concentrations and variety of big game our modern world has known without witnessing any of that excellence. There were occasional ostriches that dashed off, as if suddenly remembering a quieter spot over the horizon. There were gazelles, sprightly in their step and flicking their tails behind them, as well as zebras, squat and dumpy compared with horses; but of the great herds, not a thing. They, as many other people kept telling me, were best seen in the parks, even those many years ago.

Luckily, I was able to revisit Africa a few years later as a journalist at a conservation conference. Spurred by the Gold Coast, which had become independent Ghana, other colonial countries had sought—or were seeking—independence. The ruling foreigners, by and large, were accepting the inevitable, but they did wonder about its consequences. They certainly worried about the animals. What would happen to the majestic herds and all the precious parks when Europeans relinquished control of the continent to the Africans? A meeting was proposed for all interested parties to discuss this point. Would independence mean a sudden ending for the game, a conclusion for wildlife? Or was optimism possible?

The conference of 1961, in Arusha—capital of Tanganyika's northern province—was planned as the largest of its kind. In theory 25 African countries were to be represented, but several could not afford the fare. In actuality 140 participants from 21 African countries attended. White faces far outnumbered black ones. The location was significant; northern Tanganyika possessed the greatest herds. The timing was critical; African nations had recently gained liberty or were working toward it. Of extra and unforeseen significance was a drought, then at its most extreme and the worst on record since the previous century. Hundreds of thousands of cattle were dying, and wild animals were also in trouble. A daunting prospect for the gathered conservationists was that pastoralists might invade the parks in search of better grasses, boreholes that supplied good water, or land that had once been theirs.

The tremendous Serengeti, possibly Africa's most famous park, was a particularly contentious issue. When it had been created in 1951, the Masai pastoralists living in it had been evicted, *(Continued on page 30)*

Sanctuaries of
East Africa

FOLLOWING PAGES: Jaws agape, a crocodile lunges at wildebeests crowding the banks of the Grumeti River in Tanzania's Serengeti National Park. Along East Africa's Great Rift Valley lie some of the continent's greatest wildlife reserves.

Stripes stand out when plains zebras pause, but they camouflage the animals and confuse predators as the zebras move through grasses. Elephants glory in lush lowland vegetation around watering holes in Kenya's Amboseli National Park. In East Africa's reserves, where big-game hunters once took trophies, visitors now amass photographs. Researchers conducting long-term studies at Amboseli garner knowledge of elephants' social and communications systems that may help secure their future.
FOLLOWING PAGES: Baring enormous fangs, a testy lioness drives a bothersome cub from her kill in Masai Mara National Reserve.

Secure within their pride, lions snooze in a heap in Masai Mara. Two lively cubs stalk a littermate, honing hunting skills. The big predators play an important role in maintaining balance in park wildlife populations. Kenya's burgeoning human population—it grows 3.5 percent a year—pushes small farmers and pastoralists ever closer to such sanctuaries. Conservationists seek ways to make local people benefit directly from their wildlife heritage so that they will take an active interest in protecting it.
FOLLOWING PAGES: Scrambling to keep up, a giraffe trails its long-legged mother. Browsing high in trees, the lanky creatures take advantage of food inaccessible to shorter herbivores.

*F*eeding above their reflections, lesser flamingos crowd Lake Nakuru,
the first Kenyan reserve established primarily for birds. White pelicans
gather along the shore of the alkaline waters. A tawny eagle glares
from its perch. Numerous birds depend on such lakes for food, but population
pressure and urban expansion threaten the quality of their water.
FOLLOWING PAGES: Cheetahs share a Thomson's gazelle, a common
prey of the swift cats. Other predators often poach from cheetahs.

Africa

mainly to the area around and within the equally well-known Ngorongoro Crater. This largest caldera in Africa was the home of thousands of wild animals—notably wildebeests, zebras, lions, elephants, and rhinoceroses. Rhinos were specifically and intensely debated at the conference. Not only were they dying from the drought, but some had also been speared. Hundreds of thousands of cattle had recently died in Masai land, but the delegates spent more time discussing rhinos, aware that, by killing them, the Masai had been expressing discontent in their traditional style. The dead animals' horns had not been removed—that was not the Masai way. These people had announced most tellingly that they, too, had a point of view, and rights, and a way of life to be preserved.

Little emphasized in the schoolroom used for the 1961 conference was that Africa's people and animals had formerly coexisted. Contrary to what has been frequently (and most sentimentally) suggested, the relationship was not totally harmonious. Human lives or interests were sometimes imperiled by wildlife; the words "meat" and "animal" often shared the same root (in Swahili, for example); but the colossal herds that so astonished Europeans on their initial forays into the continent had lived alongside human beings successfully. Africa had been preeminent in this regard, and the stewardship of its animal inheritance had been astonishing. But the possibility of continued coexistence was not addressed at Arusha. Africans, it was generally considered, could not be trusted with their wildlife. Parks empty of people were the only safeguard, as evidenced by all the enclaves forged by the Belgians, British, French, and Portuguese in their various colonies.

The Africans could have pointed out, had their delegates been more numerous or outspoken, that the great slaughtering of big game occurred only after the old ways had been disrupted. Killing for sport had been introduced, along with destructive weaponry. Rinderpest flourished under the new order as people and their animals were moved, and imported, large-scale agricultural techniques proved alien to human and animal coexistence. Moreover, the regions regaining independence would not be reacquiring what had existed formerly because the world had changed so much since colonization.

Few delegates at Arusha believed any form of partnership might have merit. Instead there was a general consensus that parks could not include any kind of pastoralist—not even the Masai, whose lifestyle apparently had remained unaltered since their forebears first entered the Serengeti Plain. No wonder that grievances had surfaced, with a few speared rhinos affirming the degree of discontent. To some people, these protests seemed to prove that Africans could never again exist with wildlife. Parks were the solution, denuded of people, strictly reserved for animals—and for visitors who would pay.

In 1961 there were only a few such parks in Tanganyika: notably Serengeti and Lake Manyara. There was also the Ngorongoro

Kenyan park rangers guard 2,500 elephant tusks confiscated from poachers. An international accord banning trade in raw ivory produced a decline in the slaughter of elephants, but shrinking habitat still threatens their survival.

Conservation Area, but it was not considered a "proper" park because people lived there, including some who had been expelled from the Serengeti. Masai were grazing cattle and building circular manyattas even within the region's showpiece, the 100-square-mile crater encircled by walls 2,000 feet high. This natural amphitheater was home to more than 9,000 big game animals, 7,000 cattle, and, as I remember seeing at the time, 3 very sick rhinos gashed by spears. For my newspaper I wrote that these wounds were "a small thing, maybe, in a period of nuclear tests and nuclear capabilities, but symptomatic of the fact that the most remarkable natural zoo on Earth was in danger of being destroyed."

The Arusha delegates were no less pessimistic, whether at the school or in the field. Tanganyika was to become the 29th independent African state. Its people prepared to rejoice accordingly, but the future of the wildlife appeared distinctly bleak. The new country initially let the Masai continue to live in the crater. In time, however, these cattle-lovers were displaced, and tourists were allowed to camp on the hallowed ground. Although their safari tents were discreetly situated, eventually the campers, too, were asked to leave; only daytime visits were allowed.

When I last saw Ngorongoro Crater, in 1993, it looked magnificent. Its vastness dwarfed visiting vehicles. There were at least 12

Africa

rhinos in residence, all in good shape and none with a spear wound in its flank. More importantly, additional parks had been gazetted in the country now called Tanzania, bringing the number to 12 and more than doubling the acreage of parkland it had inherited from anxious colonials. The country has had a difficult time politically, but 15 percent of its territory overall is now officially protected within some form of reservation.

Like a messenger from a distant war, one delegate to Arusha arrived with important news from the former Belgian Congo. Everyone knew of the turmoil occurring in that country, a turbulence precipitated by hasty independence and general unpreparedness. Everyone at Arusha wished to hear how the parks and their inhabitants were faring, notably the mountain gorillas first made famous by a young zoologist named George Schaller. He had pioneered a style of observation characterized by objectivity and meticulous zeal. Photographs showing Schaller and his wife in relaxed fashion observing, and being casually observed by, the largest of the apes were quite unparalleled. The news from the Congo brought by Jacques Verschuren was troubling. There had been, he told us, terrific fights between park rangers and park invaders, with deaths on both sides. "Are the animals safe?" one ranger had asked, as he lay dying from a spear wound. He had closed his eyes, seemingly at peace, after hearing that 450 mountain gorillas living at an elevation of about 10,000 feet had not suffered the deadly fate of lowland gorillas.

I was able to visit that area in 1963 and see it for myself. Schaller's research hut at Kabara in the old Albert National Park (now Virunga National Park) had been burned. His researched animals were more wary of humans, but many groups still lived among the moss-covered *Hagenia* woodland of that extraordinary environment. Their shrieks of warning as I approached effectively stopped—I will swear—every corpuscle in my body, but subsequent sightings of the animals were as magical as could be.

The Virunga area then became Dian Fossey territory. For 18 years she fought desperately for the gorillas and eventually was killed. Visitors have contributed money, before and after her death, for the chance to see these supreme animals, preferring them to the more abundant lowland variety, but these happy occasions have often been followed by further human tumult. In 1994, terrifying slaughter erupted in Rwanda, whose Virunga Mountains were home to half the mountain gorilla population. Wildlife inevitably assumes a lesser priority when people are at risk; but so far, despite the many wars, the increasing human population, and growing pressure for more land, both kinds of African gorillas have managed to survive—or have been permitted to survive. Good fortune, good management, and able concern have come their way in the past, and hopefully sufficient luck, skill, and care will attend them in the future.

As for the Serengeti, its magnificent herds have increased in number several times since those lugubrious days when so many feared that it might not even survive. Wildebeests still migrate beyond the park's borders, and into Kenya. There are now more than a million of these animals, together with hundreds of thousands of zebras and gazelles. There is still poaching—or hunting, as those involved prefer to call their trade. There is still great loss of life as the migrants encounter the age-old natural obstacles of rivers, predators, and drought, but few delegates at that conference in 1961 could have foreseen such a future. "We will do everything in our power to make sure that our children's grandchildren will be able to enjoy this rich and precious inheritance," affirmed Tanzania's leaders after that assembly. Their children's children are doing so already, and the grandchildren to come will surely do so soon.

Outsiders with expertise and cash can and do assist. More than half a million tourists a year visit Kenya, a number that would shrink dramatically if its parks disappeared. The imported money is significant, but the continent as a whole, which receives 18 million visitors a year, grows increasingly delighted by its wild inheritance. When initiating parks, the former colonials managed to alienate most Africans by making them think of wildlife as just another form of foreign preserve. The current sight of minibuses loaded with white faces does not necessarily dispel that view, but a pride in Africa is growing steadily.

"You came all this way just to see monkeys?" asked a man I met recently in Uganda's Kibale Forest. About 1,400 primates live in each square mile of the forest; it has the densest primate population of any place in the world. "Yes," I answered, "and very happily." He gazed again at the 17 animals feeding on a single fig tree, as if seeing them for the first time.

Unfortunately, even if parks are no longer viewed as colonial remnants, they can still be regarded as emblems of authority, administered by a government that may or may not be popular. After Ethiopia's socialist regime was toppled in 1991, its Bale Mountains National Park—home of the mountain nyala, Simien jackal, and giant mole rat—was viciously attacked. Administrative buildings were damaged, and animals were butchered out of revenge for the previous system rather than out of a need for meat or to show resentment against conservation. The new government is making sincere attempts at conservation.

Africa's well-known magazine *Drum* started in the 1950s with a feature called "Your Tribal Music." Gradually perceptions changed, and "Our Music" replaced it. Now it is called "Drumbeat." This change in attitude is reflected in park management. Parks and animals are African— as African as can be—along with the people who share the continent with them. They do not belong to any government, beneficent or otherwise.

One overriding problem exhibits few signs of vanishing or even lessening: Africa's human numbers are increasing rapidly. Despite lethal coups, disease, and considerable malnutrition, the population increases relentlessly year after year. A 70-year-old Kenyan may have 8 children, 50 grandchildren, and 180 great-grandchildren. Nairobi, Kenya's capital, was wilderness a century ago. Now it has 2 million people, a disturbing crime

Africa

rate, great poverty, and frightening unemployment. Demand for nearby land is fearsome, with even marginal territory being stripped bare.

In 1963, when I first visited Lake Nakuru National Park, a reserve northwest of Nairobi known for its flamingos, I had to ask where its borders lay. There is no need now for such a question because the boundary fence is marked in places by laundry hanging on it. In the old days it was easy to wonder why the entrance post to the Ngorongoro Conservation Area had been located, apparently at random, in the middle of a forest. This is no longer a mystery. Agricultural plots, interspersed with the rectangular dwellings of those who plant and eat the crops, now lead right to the forest's edge, where the entrance post stands—guardian of a reserve beginning as abruptly as any ocean takes over from the land. "What wisdom," a visitor may mutter, "for reserves and parks to have been established before it was too late." This same visitor might then mumble, "What skill and acumen will be required to sustain the effects of such forethought from obliteration because human numbers were not curtailed."

Such wantonness, fortunately, has not yet occurred, even though a 3.5 percent growth rate, as in Kenya, is alarming. Indeed, reserves are still being created. Tanzania's Udzungwa Mountain National Park was gazetted only in 1992. The Republic of Congo's second national park, Nouabalé-Ndoki, was formally declared in 1993 (the first was established during French rule in 1940). The Congo legislation was all the more remarkable for occurring during major unrest within the country. Elections had been disputed by a frustrated opposition, and guns had been fired on the streets

Giants of the insect world, goliath beetles span the hand of a boy in Zaire's Virunga National Park. Collecting butterflies and intriguing invertebrates such as the beetles may afford local residents extra income.

of the capital, Brazzaville, but despite understandable postponement the necessary paperwork eventually was signed by the president.

This new 1,490-square-mile park is particularly attractive because many of its animals, such as the chimpanzees, behaved as if human beings were not part of their experience. The animals did not flee, which is generally their wisest course. Instead they stood their ground; they were even curious. Plainly, this was an area that had to be conserved, whether peace or war prevailed. Such pristine wilderness, even in a continent with only 56 people to each square mile, is rare and exceedingly dear. Nouabalé-Ndoki has been called "the last Eden" for good reason. Foresters and developers have been busy elsewhere, much to the benefit of this park's lowland gorillas, forest elephants, bongos, sitatungas, leopards, duikers, and all those fearless chimpanzees.

A most rewarding happenstance is that Congo's new park abuts the Dzanga-Sangha Reserve of the neighboring Central African Republic (C.A.R). For the most part, continental Africa's 46 countries respect their own boundaries, caring most about problems within these lines drawn almost entirely by 19th-century Europeans. Animals are oblivious to such invisible frontiers. The Congo-C.A.R. protection is therefore doubly fortunate because the parks are united, as are Tanzania's Serengeti and adjoining Masai Mara National Reserve in Kenya. Such accord is not as common as might be wished.

Fortunately, there was considerable accord over ivory. Many of Africa's parks, notably those in the central belt, had suffered terrible depredations on their elephant populations, primarily because of the world's enthusiasm for tusk products. A worldwide ban on ivory trading proved a major success. In the field of conservation, as is frequently stated, success is often a matter of preventing defeats rather than gaining victories. Although nine African countries—the most outspoken being those in southern Africa—were against the ban when it was instituted in 1989, they yielded to its imposition. As a result, the world price of ivory dropped, as did the poached supply of raw material.

When the matter was again discussed internationally, in 1992, the ban was continued only after much debate and strong opposition from some southern African countries. Though helpful because it gives elephants a respite from hunters and poachers, the ban is only part of the answer to the problem of the animals' survival. Elephants need large spaces, and although Africa has set aside land, the greatest threat to them is the fragmentation and shrinking of their habitat.

More than 2 percent of Africa is now national parkland, a fraction absolutely crucial to wildlife and many economies. All this conservation is less than a century old, but the formidable pressures from visitors and nationals are only recent. Only three carloads of tourists reached the 7,500-square-mile Kruger, South Africa's most famous park, in 1927; 65 years later 740 thousand people visited the park. Size is not necessarily

Africa

partnered by popularity. Though small, Nairobi National Park receives more visitors per each of its 44 square miles—about 3,700—than any other park in Kenya. The only certainty about parks in general is that current difficulties will grow rather than diminish. Animal territories will become more compressed; visitors will become more desperate to see the sights before they disappear; the economics of park management will become more critical. And yet the wildness must be preserved. The glory of the past must somehow remain available for the future. That, at the very least, must be delivered to our successors.

Following the motorcycle ride of my student days, and aware of a saddle's imperfections, I chose a hydrogen balloon as my next vehicle for traversing Africa. From the comfort of its basket, I had hoped to watch the great herds stroll beneath this first such craft ever to come their way. In truth, when the flights began, the romance was often difficult to detect, as great thermals treated us like thistledown. We were bounced a mile or more above the ground, and our landings were bruisingly memorable; but the magic I had foreseen existed—just occasionally. Whether we watched buffaloes thrashing in single file through a forest, skeins of flamingos flying below our basket, a single hyena or tens of thousands of wildebeests on a plain, we were happily enchanted by this world of wonders.

At the end of the trip, after a flight across Tanzania's most famous park, I wrote:

> The Serengeti is a legacy that must always be. Whatever the difficulties it must survive; its destruction is unthinkable. For anyone who imagines otherwise, let him go there, and let him be enriched by it.

That was 30 years ago, and the legacy is as precious as ever. Let us hope that it, and all the tremendous parks of tremendous Africa, do survive, so that generation after generation can be equally enriched. There is, in truth, no other way. Old, wild Africa must continue to exist—whatever the future holds.

Madagascar

Crowned lemur balances on moonscape pinnacles of eroded limestone in Madagascar's Ankarana Special Reserve. Isolated from continental Africa for some 165 million years, the world's fourth largest island nurtured a unique array of wildlife epitomized by some 40 species of lemurs. Since man's arrival on the island about A.D. 500, much of the forest and 14 lemur species have vanished. Deforestation and disastrous erosion combine with runaway population growth to threaten remaining wildlife.
FOLLOWING PAGES: Jewel-like scales stud a panther chameleon. Some 50 chameleon species—about half the world's total—are endemic to Madagascar.

Okavango

Shimmer meets shade as young elephants frolic in Chobe National Park. Ancient geology linked the Chobe area and the Makgadikgadi Pans, where an ostrich sprints across the sand, with the Okavango Delta. Bee-eaters roost in a row in the Okavango, now the world's largest inland delta. Annual flooding and rainfall swell the swamp; it expands to cover 8,500 square miles, then shrinks in the dry season. Seventeen percent of Botswana lies within parks or game reserves, but development brings conflict. Fences erected to control livestock on surrounding land block wildlife migration routes, and pending water projects threaten the delta's integrity.

Africa

Virunga Mountains

Flailing bamboo, a silverback mountain gorilla charges in Virunga National Park, an area reserved for these rare apes; researchers named the animal Mrithi. A baby cuddles safe in her mother's embrace. Security proved elusive for Mrithi; soldiers shot him in 1992 during a period of civil strife. Founded in 1925 as Albert National Park and Africa's first such reserve, Virunga in Zaire and adjacent Volcans National Park in Rwanda offer a stark lesson in the vulnerability of wildlife sanctuaries.

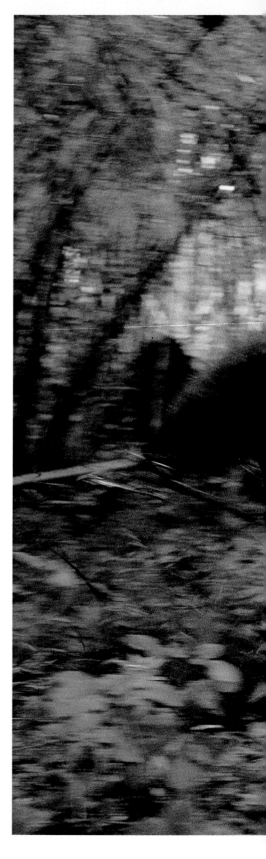

Africa

Kruger

Iridescent feathers gleaming, black storks feed in South Africa's Kruger National Park. Kudus pause at a water hole. Moving as one, two baboons eye an intruder. As wildlife dwindled in the 1880s, Paul Kruger, president of what was then the Transvaal, pioneered in setting aside the first section of the reserve that now bears his name. Arid, tropical, and subtropical zones converge in this, South Africa's oldest and largest national park, giving it a great range and variety of vegetation. Highly managed, it attracts more than 700 thousand visitors a year; largely self-supporting, it serves as a model for some African reserves.

Namib-Naukluft

*Buried in the sands of Namib-Naukluft Park, a horned adder awaits
a target for its venomous fangs. Serpentine dunes shift in sinuous curves
at the edge of a dry riverbed. Encompassing 19,200 sere square miles
in the southwest African nation of Namibia, the reserve ranks as one of the
world's biggest parks. Some of the largest dunes in the world, reaching a
thousand feet in height, lie within its confines. To preserve its wildlife
heritage, sparsely populated Namibia has established other large reserves such
as Etosha National Park and Skeleton Coast Park. The nations of Africa
have set aside more than 2 percent of the continent as parkland.*

Africa

Greater flamingos flap across the Camargue of southern France—a wet
and wild sanctuary on the edge of crowded, industrialized Europe.

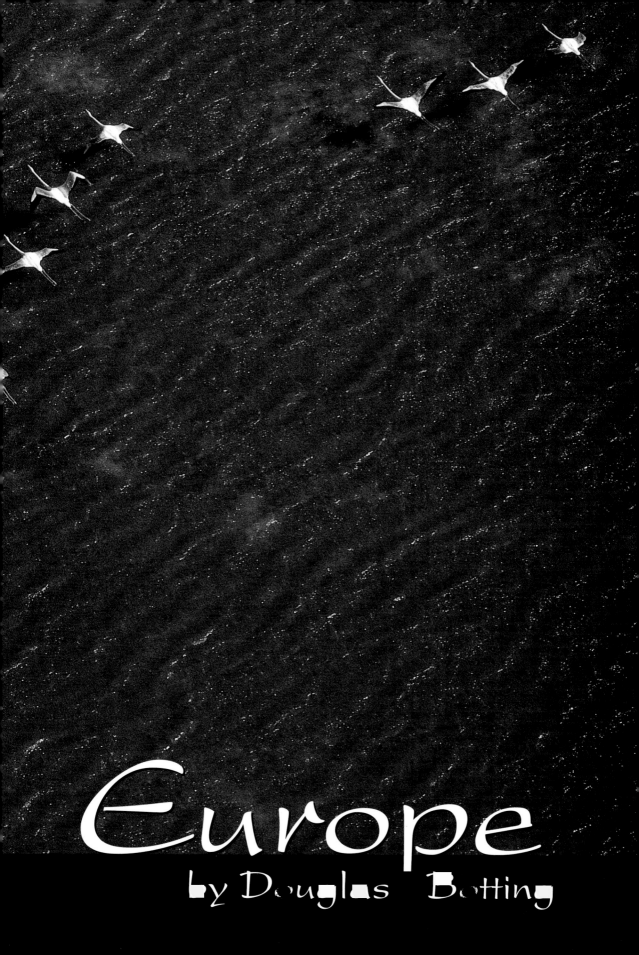

Europe

by Douglas Botting

I CAME OUT OF THE PALACIO into the blinding Andalusian sun. A placid nag stood in front of the great oak door, already saddled, with a gray-uniformed *guarda* in a broad-brimmed Spanish cowboy's sombrero holding the bridle, waiting for me to mount. Beyond both horse and ranger stretched a brown flatland of marsh and plain reaching to the horizon. Out of this breathless wilderness rose a distant and unending clamor of birds.

I eyed the nag with suspicion. I had ridden only once before, and now faced the prospect of spending an entire day in the saddle on a long trail over rough country.

"*Segunda vez,*" I explained to the ranger, who was known as Curro. "Only the second time, you know." Curro was a man of few words but a powerful voice. "*Monte, monte!*" he roared. "Get on!"

Poland's snowy Tatra National Park seems the picture of wildness—and indeed the rare eagle owl may survive here. This largest of all European owls was classed as vermin in France until the 1960s, while bounties were paid elsewhere. Now protected, it is being reintroduced into some areas.

Europe

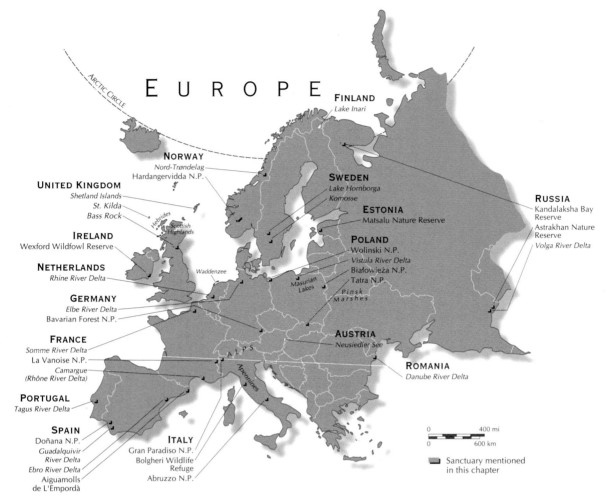

E U R O P E

ARCTIC CIRCLE

FINLAND
Lake Inari

NORWAY
Nord-Trøndelag
Hardangervidda N.P.

SWEDEN
Lake Hornborga
Komosse

UNITED KINGDOM
Shetland Islands
St. Kilda
Bass Rock
Hebrides
Scottish Highlands

ESTONIA
Matsalu Nature Reserve

RUSSIA
Kandalaksha Bay Reserve
Astrakhan Nature Reserve
Volga River Delta

IRELAND
Wexford Wildfowl Reserve

POLAND
Wolinski N.P.
Vistula River Delta
Białowieża N.P.
Tatra N.P.
Pinsk Marshes

NETHERLANDS
Rhine River Delta
Waddenzee

Masurian Lakes

GERMANY
Elbe River Delta
Bavarian Forest N.P.

FRANCE
Somme River Delta
La Vanoise N.P.
Camargue (Rhône River Delta)

ALPS

Apennines

AUSTRIA
Neusiedler See

ROMANIA
Danube River Delta

PORTUGAL
Tagus River Delta

SPAIN
Doñana N.P.
Guadalquivir River Delta
Ebro River Delta
Aiguamolls de L'Empordà

ITALY
Gran Paradiso N.P.
Bolgheri Wildlife Refuge
Abruzzo N.P.

| 0 | | 400 mi |
| 0 | | 600 km |

▬ Sanctuary mentioned in this chapter

I hauled myself into the saddle. The nag lurched into motion, aiming for the thin brown line that marked the frontier between land and sky. Soon the white ducal Palacio, once the hunting lodge of Spanish nobility, receded behind us. We were swallowed up in the expanse of Doñana National Park, also known as Coto Doñana or simply "the Coto." My eyes explored the horizon, then focused on a distant bird ascending the eastern sky, soaring with unhurried authority in wide circles on immense, outstretched raptor wings. That horseback view of a distant Spanish imperial eagle—one of Europe's rarest birds—remains a treasured memory even now, some 20 years later, well worth every tweak of pain my day in the saddle gave me. My ride that day was a privileged glimpse of a special kind of Eden in a continent where Edens are at a premium. The sky was an immense rotunda whose far horizons held us like spiders in a bell jar. The sun, the wind, and a great natural peace descended on us, broken only by the snorting of the horses, the jingling of their bits, and occasional cries from Curro as he called out the names of various species in this swooping, shrieking, skulking bird metropolis.

Doñana is one of the great wild places of Europe. It comprises 310 square miles, about half of them relatively dry: dunes, heaths, stone-pine woods, cork-oak savannas. Residents include pardel lynxes, mongooses, snakes, and big, black, aggressive bulls. A no-man's-land of seasonal marsh marks the beginning of Las Marismas (The Marshes), a vast, bird-thronged wetland that is part of the Guadalquivir River's 749-square-mile delta, on southern Spain's Atlantic coast. Part of Las Marismas is included in the national park, which harbors more than 200 species of birds, about 30 mammals, and a similar number of reptiles and amphibians.

These wetlands are a crucial junction where birds from as far away as the tropics and the polar regions rest and feed during complex seasonal migrations across three continents. Las Marismas is the most important wintering ground for ducks in all of Spain. In spring, pintails and teal and greylag geese take off for northern Europe, and wigeons go to Siberia— while egrets, white storks, bee-eaters, and hoopoes arrive from Africa to breed. I had come to Spain in June, toward the end of nesting season. Our route to Las Marismas skirted cork-oak woods teeming with spoonbills, herons, and egrets, then plunged through broad marshes packed with waterbirds of every description, from the rare and ungainly purple gallinule—with its big red beak and maniacal shriek—to throngs of breeding ducks. Birds were everywhere, some scuttling about my horse's hoofs, some staring from hummocks, others just making a hell of a hullabaloo at our uninvited intrusion.

Later, with another guide—Pepe—I would visit Lucio de Mari López, a shallow and highly saline lake where about 2,000 greater flamingos were feeding. Though they now breed only occasionally in Doñana, they still return here from Africa each summer. A prolonged grumbling came from them, like the muttering of a football crowd whose team is losing. As we drew nearer, a wave of anxiety prompted them to riffle their wings, causing the flock's color to alternate rapidly between white and brilliant pink, resulting in a roseate, vibrating haze.

"*Bonito, eh?*" exclaimed Pepe, his arm describing a wide arc that encompassed the lake and its birds, a prairie of waving grasses, and some mirage-like stone pines, all on the shimmering edge of a continent.

"*Bonito,*" I replied. Yes, it was beautiful. But would my children's children ever see this place as I had, I wondered? The birds flying free, other animals running wild in one of Europe's last great wildernesses?

In a continent as crowded and developed as this, animal sanctuaries live cheek by jowl with every other phenomenon of the late 20th century. The Coto-Marismas area of the Guadalquivir Delta constitutes one of the largest nearly intact ecosystems in southwest Europe today. It is a UNESCO biosphere reserve, and has been designated a wetland of international importance in accordance with an intergovernmental treaty known as the Ramsar Convention. It also is an example of the colliding interests that bedevil even the finest protected areas. For though it is a formal sanctuary, numerous human activities crowd its borders: burgeoning tourism, extensive rice farming and irrigation schemes, mining, hunting, fishing, cattle grazing, and road building—to name a few. At times, polluted waters have killed thousands of birds. (*Continued on page 60*)

Europe

Sanctuaries of
Europe's Wetlands

Birds and people share Europe's wetlands, not always peaceably. Starlings
flock at Lake Hornborga (above), part of a 13-square-mile wetland
in Sweden. Several attempts to drain the region for farmland ended in the
mid-1900s, about the time a conservation society purchased and set aside
Sweden's boggy Komosse—where a whooper swan (left) now stretches its wings.
On the Austria-Hungary border, a spoonbill fishes the saline shallows of
Neusiedler See, an inland lake protected from human incursion by
extensive reedbeds and marshes—as well as by official decree.
FOLLOWING PAGES: Flamingos in the Camargue turn their eggs.

Europe

Although under siege for centuries by farmers, fishermen, miners, hunters, tourists, and recreationists, Europe's wetlands persist. Many are river deltas. Where the Rhône enters the Mediterranean, the Camargue's famed white horses (below) thrive; black woolly coats at birth turn gray by four and grow progressively paler. Spain's Guadalquivir River finds the Atlantic northwest of Gibraltar. There, in Doñana National Park, a red deer (opposite) bellows after battling a rival for a doe. The park, established in 1969, occupies land used as a hunting ground by Spanish nobility for 500 years. At the confluence of migration routes between Africa and Europe, it shelters hundreds of thousands of birds.

When I visited the Coto, Dr. Javier Castroviejo, director of Doñana Biological Station, was not optimistic. "There is little we can do," he told me. " If we stop the poisoned rivers flowing into Las Marismas, the water level will drop and the wildlife will decline. If the rivers continue to flow, the wildlife will be poisoned. Either way it will one day spell the end of this wonderful place." Thankfully, that day still has not arrived.

For all its 4,000,000 square miles of diverse landscapes and 50,000 miles of highly indented coastline, Europe is the smallest continent, save for Australia. On top of that, it is densely populated. The impacts of people upon the natural face of this continent have been immense. Long ago, vast forests stretched from the Atlantic to Asia and beyond, harboring lions and fallow deer; the hills of Athens once were thickly forested in oak and pine. Successive waves of settler-farmers felled such stands and waged wars on the animals that threatened them or their livestock. Today, wildlife habitats have been overrun, with species often exterminated, marginalized, or otherwise compromised. Wolves, wolverines, Mediterranean monk seals, bears, and lynxes now have only the slenderest footholds. In Italy every year some 1.5 million licensed hunters—an army greater than the combined military forces of Britain, France, and Germany—blaze away, killing millions or perhaps hundreds of millions of migrating birds over thousands of square miles. On no other continent has nature taken such a beating.

Yet, amazingly, thousands of wild places still exist here, scattered like oases of nature in a man-made wilderness that stretches from beyond the Irish Sea to the Urals, from Arctic islands to the Mediterranean. Many enjoy official protection as national parks, nature reserves, biosphere reserves, or world heritage sites. Others have no formal status at all. The largest and most blatantly wild ones, like Lapland and the tundras and snowfields of higher mountains, usually consist of land that is too unproductive or inaccessible to farm or develop. Some, such as Doñana and the Białowieża Forest on the Poland-Belarus border, initially survived as hunting grounds of the ruling aristocracy. Others, like Bolgheri Wildlife Refuge on the northwest coast of Italy—a splendid place to see crested porcupines, wild boars, and migrant birds such as bluethroats and Blyth's reed warblers—were founded as the result of private initiative.

With the rise of the conservation movement over the last few decades, a whole galaxy of sanctuaries has been added to the list, and more are planned. It would take a lifetime to tour them all. Since 1983, a total of more than 66,000 square miles—an area nearly half the size of Germany—has been set aside. Some reserves are vast, such as Norway's 1,300-square-mile Hardangervidda National Park, which contains the largest population of reindeer in Europe. Many are tiny. Ireland's Wexford Wildfowl Reserve, for example, spans a mere 0.4 square miles—yet more than half of the world's Greenland white-fronted geese winter there every year. Europe's wildlife sanctuaries vary greatly in terrain and biodiversity, from bird-rich estuaries to the far north's lonely snowfields, from the green gloom of surviving forests to the scorching plains of Spain's tablelands.

My own recollections of such places comprise a kaleidoscope of images I find at once poignant, glorious, and exhilarating. Take, for example, the Scottish Highlands and the Hebrides. Not many parts of Europe can be wilder than this northwestern frontier of rock and sea. While several places here are designated sanctuaries, in a sense the entire area constitutes one great repository of animal life. Its human population is small, with many islands uninhabited. The most far-flung and spectacular of the Hebrides, St. Kilda, comprises a handful of storm-wracked islets that boast the oldest fulmar colony in Britain and the biggest gannet colony in the world—as well as a unique little wren, a unique little mouse, and the mouflon-like Soay sheep.

On the West Highland coast, I especially recall one magical night spent in a blanket amid the dunes of a little bay called Sandaig. The ocean was softly bathed in moonshine to the very edge of vision. I lay for a long time staring at the full moon's bright white disk in the starlit sky and listening to the strange, wild cries of night—the *kraak* of a solitary heron stalking fish at the edge of the shore; a seal singing plaintively, its childlike voice rising and falling like a lullaby in the dark.

Then there is Europe's rugged heart, the daunting Alps, home to some 1,200 glaciers—and some of the continent's finest wildlife reserves. In 1975 I visited Italy's Gran Paradiso National Park, which abuts France's La Vanoise National Park, to look for the ibex for which the region is famous. I had climbed to about 7,000 feet and had paused on a large, flat-topped boulder to have lunch and to scan the neighboring slopes with my binoculars. No ibex.

I took out my magnifying glass and examined my lunching site from a distance of about an inch. The shift in perspective dramatically altered my perception of Gran Paradiso. Before me surged the micro-world of the Alps: Ants, like dromedaries in long caravans, bore sandwich crumbs through jungles of lichens and mosses; purplish wildflowers rose up amid big, thick, artichoke-like leaves. A trickle of meltwater gleamed with innumerable fragments of colorful schists, quartzes, and gneisses that had been chipped and pried from the great peaks all around.

I sat up, blinked, and again changed perspective. Some 50 ibex had gathered on a nearby slope and were staring at me with the fixed gaze so typical of ruminants. Thus a lesson: In the great outdoors, wildlife often comes only to those who sit and wait. I marveled at the animals' hefty haunches and scimitar-shaped horns, up to three feet long. Essentially mountain goats, ibex have survived in the Alps thanks to conservation efforts over the last century and a half; today, some 3,500 head enjoy sanctuary in Gran Paradiso National Park.

Some 900 miles to the northeast, on the Poland-Belarus border, the bison of Białowieża Forest have returned from the brink of extinction. Largely a woodland creature, the wisent, or European bison, fared badly

Europe

as the continent became deforested; the last wild one was shot in the Caucasus in 1927. Two years later, work began on a project to eventually restore bison to the wild, through captive breeding and release of zoo animals. Today, about 500 of these magnificent creatures roam the woods of Białowieża. Adult bulls stand nearly six feet high and weigh almost a ton, can charge at thirty miles an hour and jump over a six-foot fence.

Białowieża's virtually primeval forest also shelters both red and roe deer, boars, wolves, lynxes, otters, and foxes—as well as beavers and polecats. Visitors here can see a slice of Europe as it existed thousands of years ago. Some of these oaks and pines, in fact, were saplings when Shakespeare wrote *Hamlet*.

For me the appeal of a wildlife sanctuary is not just the wildlife but the wild land as well—ibex scrambling high in Gran Paradiso, geese heading south over the narrows of Skye, frogs moving like an army through the primeval woods of Białowieża. Yet recently, in the rural but very *un*wild shire of Suffolk, England, I saw a spectacular wildlife display: butterflies, the biggest congregation I'd ever experienced anywhere.

England's butterflies have had a hard time, what with insecticide spraying and habitat disturbance, so I was astonished to come across a huge bush so entirely covered with them that nothing of the plant could be seen. There were species I had not seen in years. Only later did I learn of a possible explanation: A strong wind may have blown these butterflies across the Channel from the Continent, taken them inland to the hamlet of Hoxne, and lifted them over the garden wall of a medieval inn known as The Swan, where they encountered a huge buddleia bush in full flower—manna from heaven. Thus this enormous swarm had found a sanctuary that was neither primeval marsh nor remote Alpine meadow, merely the garden of a village pub. It was a sanctuary only because local humans no longer rush at butterflies with nets and insecticides, but choose instead to stand back and admire. In a modern world overrun by people, wildlife's survival depends largely on human states of mind.

Europe's wetlands have been both crowning glory and recurring shame. Few other European habitats can rival their sheer prodigality of wildlife. The best ones—the great bird marshes of some southern river deltas, for example—still harbor post-Ice Age scenes of exuberant, unspoiled nature. Yet many have been destroyed, while others are increasingly threatened. In Britain's Great Fens, where spoonbills and glossy ibis once waded beneath the soaring spire of Ely Cathedral, wheat now ripens. Some 95 percent of Worcestershire's marshlands have disappeared since World War II. Italy's Mussolini drained the famous Pontine Marshes of Rome—once the vast and wild haunt of boars, foxes, and myriad birds—before a comprehensive study of resident wildlife could be made. Greece has lost half of its wetlands in this century. Spain has managed to save Las Marismas—but excessive pumping of groundwater has sounded the death knell for its

Tablas de Daimiel marshland. The sad fact is that even protected wetlands remain under constant pressure from factors outside their boundaries. Nearby agriculture, urbanization, industrialization, mass tourism, pollution, dam building, hunting, and overfishing all continue to take their toll. That so many wetland areas persist is a measure of their original extent, as well as of the conservation community's successes.

Of 726 internationally important wetland sites currently listed by the Ramsar Convention, more than half are in Europe. They comprise a host of different types and sizes. Many serve as stepping-stones for migratory birds bound from the Arctic to Africa or Asia and back. By the hundreds of thousands, these avian commuters clock through different wetlands like jet-setting club-class passengers looking for a drink and an overnight stop. Near the mouth of the Vistula on Poland's Baltic seaboard, for example, one bird-watcher counted nearly a hundred separate species during a single visit, including 19 kinds of ducks, 14 different raptors, and 16 varieties of waders.

Europe's far north—much of it the remote and largely uninhabited forests and tundras of Scandinavia—ranks as premier wilderness. Finland alone boasts some 62,000 lakes, among them vast, marsh-fringed Lake Inari, with important populations of ducks and other birds. Its forested banks shelter bears, wolves, and wolverines. Remoteness from sizable human populations enables such sites to remain relatively pristine, for Inari enjoys no formal protection, and local Lapps hunt freely there. On the northern coast of Russia's White Sea, 800-square-mile Kandalaksha Bay Reserve harbors a mix of sea islands, coastal meadows, sedge beds, and part of the world's largest forest: the great Russian taiga. Its inventory includes 23 terrestrial mammals, 10 marine mammals, and 210 birds.

From the Arctic southward, a sequence of Atlantic coastal habitats stretches for some 3,500 miles all the way to southern Spain and Portugal. Many of these areas are river deltas: Germany's Elbe, the Netherlands' Rhine, France's Somme, and Portugal's Tagus. Some are buttressed by soaring cliffs; others, such as the Waddenzee, are largely mudflats. The Waddenzee is one of Europe's most precious wetland areas, and one of particular concern. The northeast Atlantic is difficult to protect, because fishing interests, coastal development, and offshore industries often are at loggerheads with conservationists.

Ecosystems also are suffering in the nearly landlocked Baltic, one of the world's smallest and most polluted seas. Even so, armadas of water birds congregate here. The Matsalu Nature Reserve on Estonia's coast— a major wetland of some 187 square miles—is known especially for the delicate arctic terns that seasonally trek from Arctic to Antarctic realms, migrating farther than any other animal. At the mouth of the Oder River on Poland's western frontier, Wolinski National Park shelters breeding populations of white-tailed eagles.

Europe's most extensive swamplands lie well inland, along the taiga's glacier-scoured southern edge. They include Poland's Masurian

Europe

Lakes and the Pinsk Marshes of Belarus and Ukraine. While some areas have been hunted out or turned into tourist resorts, a good number have become sanctuaries—for reintroduced beavers, for ospreys, for sea eagles, and for a host of waterfowl that includes the world's largest concentration of mute swans. Farther south and west, in Hungary, a flat and nearly treeless swath known as the *puszta*, or plain, contains numerous steppe lakes, shallow but rich in birdlife. Dotting the country from one end to the other, these lakes are as important as Scandinavia's lowlands and the great river deltas. One of them, Neusiedler See, claims 300 bird species of record, including Europe's largest colony of great white herons.

The Danube, second in length only to the Volga, meanders past ten countries as it descends from Germany's Black Forest to the Black Sea. Though this river is polluted and its banks are often intensively cultivated, it remains one of the continent's richest fonts of wildlife, in effect a linear sanctuary. Its 2,000-square-mile delta, larger than Spain's Doñana and France's Camargue combined, stands out as one of Europe's greatest wetlands. Every year, in fact, it grows about a hundred feet longer, thanks to annual additions of millions of tons of riverborne silt.

Both a biosphere reserve and a Ramsar site, the Danube Delta boasts numerous nature reserves. Its sprawl of reedbeds, freshwater lakes, and river channels shelters 280 bird species, including nesting populations of glossy ibis and rare Dalmatian pelicans. About 24 kinds of reptiles and amphibians also live here, while resident mammals include wolves, otters, minks, muskrats, steppe polecats, and raccoon dogs.

In the latter years of the Ceauşescu regime, Romania planned to canalize and drain some of this delta's most productive marshes for agriculture. That regime's downfall has put such schemes on hold, and a management plan is now being prepared for the Danube Delta Biosphere Reserve. Yet in Russia's equally important Volga Delta, conservationists fear that the morass of administrative and economic problems spawned by the Soviet Union's collapse actually may paralyze any attempts to undo existing ecological threats. The Volga suffers from dams, large-scale agricultural reclamation projects, and intensive bird hunting. It draws between five and seven million waterfowl, as well as many other birds, marsh frogs by the million, Caspian seals, and saiga antelopes. Its core sanctuary is the 244-square-mile Astrakhan Nature Reserve, one of the oldest reserves in the former U.S.S.R.

The pressures of development and pollution tend to be more intense in southern and coastal wetlands than in northern, inland ones; Mediterranean wetlands are the most threatened of all. Partly this is due to lack of funds and commitments from governments there, partly to the fact that such ecosystems extend into North African or Middle Eastern domains, where conservation laws often are nonexistent or not enforced. Spain has been desertified by both man and nature for centuries. Perhaps no other nation in Western Europe has suffered so much from erosion. Yet it still has bears and wolves, lammergeiers and great bustards, and hundreds of other species. In some ways, Spain remains the wildest European country south of the Arctic Circle. Its natural park of Aiguamolls de L'Empordà in Catalonia boasts extensive marshes and grasslands that support some 300 bird species, 11 different bats, and varied amphibians and reptiles such as three-toed skinks, spiny-footed lizards, stripe-necked terrapins, and Montpellier snakes. To the south and west, the Ebro Delta's 120 square miles of lagoons, dunes, basins, and flats hold equally rich wildlife arrays.

As a European, I am especially aware of Western civilization's many gifts to the world. I also know that no continent has been more ravaged by war, more polarized by revolution and counterrevolution, more agonized by totalitarian genocide. No part of the planet's natural inheritance has been more ransacked than that of the continent where I was born, grew up, and continue to live. In mid-1994, the BBC news sadly pronounced the once common corncrake—a shy little bird of hayfields and meadows—extinct in Northern Ireland. Then a friend telephoned from the Scottish Highlands to say that almost no salmon were in the River Dee that summer, and hardly any grouse on nearby moors. Fished out, shot out, he thought. Scotland without salmon or grouse is like Alaska without moose.

What will be left of our wild places and our biodiversity? A Venus de Milo we can copy, a Chartres Cathedral we can rebuild. We can even reintroduce captive animals into the wild, as Bialowieża has shown. But how can we re-create a living thing that has ceased to exist? And how can we dissociate the fate of other species from the fate of our own? I recall a long-ago conversation with Dr. Castroviejo of Doñana Biological Station, after his assistant had brought in the shattered remains of a relatively rare spur-thighed tortoise that had been run over by a car.

"Poor animal!" he exclaimed. "Nobody's fault, really. It's just that the car and the tortoise were incompatible, and you can see who won."

Later, he would add, "People say, what does it matter—a few ducks having a hard time? What about all the people in the world who are having a hard time? And I say to them, it *does* matter. Because all life is related, all things are connected. The fact that we are human beings does not mean that we are separate from the other living things of this planet. If we are prepared to let the creatures of the Coto die, then we are ultimately prepared to let people die, too."

Indeed, even one's backyard can be a sanctuary for some displaced creatures of the wild. Witness the efforts of Maj. Tony Crease of the Royal Scots Dragoon Guards to transform 28 acres of what was once army land into a haven for at least 58 species of breeding birds and an extraordinary variety of plant life. From such small victories an entire war can be won.

Much of what we have done we can also undo. Thanks to legislation against river pollution and to the efforts of a few very dedicated people, the once threatened otter has returned to the upper reaches of the

Europe

Thames River, after a long exile. In the Glen Affric region of the Scottish Highlands, unique flora and fauna survive amid one of the few remaining fragments of ancient Caledonian forest. There are plans afoot to restore the same native species over a 600-square-mile area, and to eventually reintroduce long-vanished animal inhabitants such as wolves, beavers, bears, and wild boars.

Alan Watson, executive director of Trees for Life, a key organization in this particular project, commented recently:

"I believe that one of the major tasks for humanity in the next century will be to heal the damage we've done to Earth. It's not enough just to stop any further environmental degradation from taking place—for there to be a healthy planet … the destruction which has already taken place must be reversed. We need to start now, with large-scale pilot projects like this to research and demonstrate techniques … which could be relevant not just to the Highlands of Scotland, but also to other biologically degraded parts of the world—such as the Sahel region of Africa, and logged-over areas of tropical rain forest."

Already, the advent of the European Community has brought a new rigor to both visualizing and implementing conservation plans. The collapse of communism eventually may bring a peace dividend of reduced military activity and relatively stable human populations—changes that should benefit conservation. For the first time, the International Union for the Conservation of Nature is proposing an integrated, continent-wide approach to shielding Europe's wildlife and wild places. Its recent action plan reads, "protecting individual species, or even individual sites, is not enough. It calls for a shift in conservation policy—from species to habitats, from sites to ecosystems, and from national to international measures." True progress demands that we no longer view wildlife reserves as separate "islands"; they need to be linked, perhaps through protected corridors that facilitate animal migrations and the dispersion of plants.

One test of any plan's effectiveness will be the fate of Europe's most threatened species. Are we Europeans, who have despoiled so many habitats and decimated so much wildlife, at last beginning to value and honor our natural heritage? If so, then perhaps even the wolf, long our most feared competitor and most enduring symbol of wildness, may find true sanctuary. Some day—soon, I hope—its primeval howl may resound again in the Highland night: proud, defiant, and back!

Bavarian Forest

Seemingly aloof, a European lynx surveys a shrinking domain from within Germany's Bavarian Forest National Park. Waldsterben—forest death—imperils the park's 50 square miles, as acid rain causes trees to drop leaves early and die prematurely, thus degrading the lynx's woodland habitat.

Europe

Shetland Islands and Bass Rock

Tiny, privately owned Bass Rock in Scotland's Firth of Forth (opposite) harbors one of the world's largest gannet colonies, a swarming, cackling maelstrom of some 20,000 squabbling (below), mating, and nesting pairs. Their racket, according to one authority, "has few equals in nature." About 70 percent of the world's gannets flock to cliff ledges of the British Isles' 20-odd gannetries. Bringing home the aquatic bacon, a puffin (above) settles toward its burrow on Foula, in the Shetland Islands.

Europe

Białowieża

Its last wild forebear killed in 1927, this European bison running free in Białowieża National Park descends from zoo animals

reintroduced two years later. Once the private hunting reserve of princes, Białowieża's oak-and-spruce forest on the Belarus-Poland border was never heavily populated by man.

Abruzzo and Gran Paradiso

Wolves—famed in Italy as the species that succored Romulus and Remus—find sanctuary in 154-square-mile Abruzzo National Park, just two hours from Rome. High in the Apennines, Abruzzo encompasses some of Italy's most beautiful—and wildest—country. The Alps enfold another Italian national park: Gran Paradiso (below) grew from a reserve established by King Victor Emmanuel II to protect the last of Europe's ibex. Today, some 3,500 range this park.

Nord-Trøndelag
(Overleaf) ▷

Born free on a continent increasingly cluttered by man, an arctic fox in rural Norway looks over its shoulder—as well it might. Physical remoteness no longer guarantees wildness in today's world. Still, new generations of concerned conservationists, politicians, and others strive to protect Europe's diverse bounty of wildlife sanctuaries.

Europe

Lounging tigress and her cub nuzzle a greeting in Ranthambhore National Park, where teeming India struggles to save room for earth's mightiest cats.

Asia
by Patrick R. Booz

IN THE PALEST LIGHT OF EARLY DAWN, I jerked backward, then forward, as my elephant lumbered to its feet, paused for an instant, and strode forward at the sharp command of the mahout astride its neck. The low buildings of the park ranger station faded into darkness behind us. The world was silent except for the swishing of high grasses against my legs and the first cries of hidden birds. I felt a strange mixture of peace and taut expectation. All seemed tranquil and serene, yet I sensed danger lurking close at hand. As if reading my feelings, the gentle beast beneath me pushed through a particularly tall stand of elephant grass to emerge abruptly into a swampy clearing known as a *bheel*.

Before me, massive and menacing, was a mother rhinoceros. Behind her, barely visible, was her calf—a tiny gray blimp on four stalks. Hornless, peering cautiously with liquid eyes, the baby was as vulnerable

*Deep and dark, the forests of northern Borneo's Kinabalu Park harbor
a thousand kinds of orchids and a wide variety of wildlife.
East of Kinabalu an orangutan swings on a liana at Sepilok Reserve, where
foundlings and confiscated pets prepare for a return to the wild.*

Asia

as its mother was threatening. She swung toward us, her head low, and took two steps. No more were necessary. If an elephant could mince, that's what mine did, retreating gingerly behind the curtain of grass.

Here on the plains of Kaziranga National Park in northeast India, I had come face to face with one of the animal world's masterpieces, a creature described by Marco Polo nearly seven hundred years ago, though he believed it to be the mythical unicorn: "They have a single large horn in the middle of their forehead.... They have a head like a wild boar's and always carry it stooped towards the ground....They spend their time by preference wallowing in mud and slime." The Indian rhinoceros (*Rhinoceros unicornis*), so long a creature of myth, so recently brought to the edge of extinction, lives and multiplies now in some safety in a string of wildlife reserves that run from east to west in the shadow of Asia's Himalaya. These sanctuaries—Kaziranga, Royal Manas National Park in southern Bhutan, Royal Chitwan National Park in Nepal—represent the last hope of rhinos and of a breathtaking range of other wildlife.

In Kaziranga, a wildlife sanctuary since 1950, the mighty Brahmaputra River defines the flat terrain. The river, named "son of

Brahma," the Hindu god of creation, rises on the Plateau of Tibet far to the north and west, slices through the Himalaya, and runs along the reserve's northern section to create vast, marshy areas. This is the wet, grassy home of rhino, tiger, and less famous South Asian creatures—the gavial and the langur, the monitor lizard and the king cobra, the swamp deer and the barking deer, the hog deer and the sambar, the last a remarkably handsome beast with strong, three-pointed antlers and shaggy, coarse hair at the throat. Sadly, the park has a remnant of only 30-40 sambars. During a solitary walk in the withering heat of midday along a pungent backwash of the Brahmaputra, I spied a gavial, a long-snouted, fish-eating crocodile, cruising placidly. With only its nostrils and eyes poking above the surface of the water, this knobbly denizen of rivers and pools looked like the cartoon image of a toothy predator.

It is the rhinoceros that draws visitors to Kaziranga. Only this park and Chitwan to the west have this species in significant numbers, and only a thousand remain on earth. S. K. Sen, director of the Kaziranga park office, explained the rhino's precarious hold on life to me. "In ancient times the rhinoceros was full of mystery and power, and his domain was far and wide. His habitat extended far into China, and today, apart from our rhinos here, we still have two species in the islands of Indonesia."

I could confirm his story, for I had visited Ujung Kulon National Park in far southwestern Java, last sanctuary of the one-horned Javan rhino. Perhaps 60 rhinos survive there. The World Wide Fund for Nature (WWF), an international organization devoted to conservation of the world's animals, plants, and natural environments, and the Indonesian Directorate General of Forest Protection and Nature Conservation ran a census of these rhinos. More than 30 individuals were identified by their shoulder height, horn shape, eye wrinkles, and scars. The last of the three Asian species (Africa has two) is the Sumatran rhino, which inhabits the island of Sumatra and a few other spots in Southeast Asia. There are a few hundred of these two-horned, odd-toed ungulates. Gunung Leuser National Park in Sumatra shelters most of them; it is the sole preserve in the world where orangutans, elephants, tigers, and rhinos live together.

Mr. Sen continued: "In the days of the Tang Dynasty [7th-9th centuries], Chinese reveled in the exotic, and for them the rhino was a source of the precious, the arcane, the wondrous." Those attributes still describe our fascination with and love of Asia's animals. "Tame rhinos were given as tribute and royal gifts," he explained, "but the products from these wild beasts held the attraction and the reward. Rhinoceros horns became medicine and an antidote to poisons and were carved into boxes, bracelets, and chopsticks, weights for curtains, even plaques for girdles of high officials. The horns, when shaped into wish-fulfilling wands, were held by Buddhist priests when they gave their sermons."

This description of old habits of exploitation helps explain the grave danger poaching presents for so-called protected animals today. Many people desire esoteric items and find *(Continued on page 89)*

Asia

Sanctuaries of
Northern
Jndia

*Hear no evil, speak no evil seems
an apt pose for India's sacred
monkeys.* Entellus *langurs,
like these in Ranthambhore,
helped divine Rama in the Hindu
epic* The Ramayana. *Believers
offer langurs the fruit of their
gardens—and even of their tables.
The pangolin (below) forages
at night; humans see this scaly
anteater most often as a captive.
FOLLOWING PAGES: Jaws
cocked, club-snouted gavials rear
at the Kukrail Crocodile Breeding
Centre, one of nine sanctuaries
in which the endangered
crocodilian has made huge gains.*

Asia

*W*ary chital deer slake their thirst at a water hole in India's Sariska
National Park. The deer, numerous and widespread, never roam
far from water. They benefit from their association with langurs.
When the monkeys pick tree fruits, chital cluster below them and harvest their
debris. Insect host and insect eater team up for mutual benefit in Bandhavgarh
National Park: A gaur, largest of the world's wild cattle, tilts its awesome head,
and a drongo grazes on insects that infest the bull's nostrils. Once a royal
stronghold, Bandhavgarh offers more than sightings of gaur. Radio-dispatched
elephants carry visitors to view tigers that find shelter in the park.

special power in abstruse animal products. For them, tiger bone in medicaments promises strength and longevity, rhinoceros horn intensifies male potency, and, grotesquely, panda pelts confer status.

For naturalists and tourists alike, the superstar aura that surrounds rhinos and tigers in South Asia and pandas in China creates a temptation to save the glamorous creatures to the neglect of others. But the lessons of decades of wildlife conservation and ecological insight point to the overwhelming need to preserve whole habitats, entire zones with their indescribably rich interplay of plants, earth, water, and animals. The watchword today is biodiversity, and I came to appreciate the term fully only after meeting Christopher Hails at WWF headquarters in Gland, Switzerland. Hails is Programme Director of WWF, and his energy, good nature, and deep concern are infectious.

"You see," he told me, "biological diversity is the culmination of our whole planet's evolution, the result of four billion years of trial and error, the genetic gift that lives today on our unique planet. Yet it's more than just genes and species in the jungle. Biological diversity exists wherever life has taken hold, even in deserts and seas, hot sulfur springs, and on the slopes of the Himalaya. In Asia, the challenge is greatest for preserving diversity; here is where we have a large part of the world's 1.5 million described species of living organisms, and here the threat of human population pressure is greatest for the spectacular ecosystems that support those plants and animals."

Under brilliant blue skies the main range of the Himalaya glistens 50 miles to the north as the verdure of Royal Chitwan National Park embraces the rich variety of life alluded to by Chris Hails. The park spreads along Nepal's *terai* lowlands, a region of huge flat valleys known as *doons*, down-dropped areas that lie between wooded ranges. Riverine forests and grasslands and towering sal forests dominate. Sal trees soar 30 feet above the valley floor, providing cover for hog deer, chital, sambar, and barking deer. They also shelter the gaur, largest species of wild cattle in the world. Boars rut and grunt in groups of 20 or 30, fearful of the big cats—the tiger and the leopard. A grown tiger has no natural enemies, but can attack and eat leopards. Although both animals share the same land, a marvelous modus vivendi has evolved to keep their encounters to a minimum. The normally nocturnal leopards have taken increasingly to daytime hunting, while tigers maintain their nightly reign of the forests.

Each year more than a quarter of a million tourists come to Nepal. Thousands of them make their way south from Kathmandu to Chitwan,

Security blankets a newborn as it cozies up to its mother, one of an elephant
fleet that taxis tourists through India's Kanha National Park.
Tamed elephants have earned their keep in India for thousands of years.

Asia

Lugging a tranquilized panda, a farmer carries it to researchers for medical treatment in Shaanxi Province.

frequently lured by the magnificent bird life. More than 440 species of birds have been sighted in Chitwan, nearly 5 percent of all types of birds on earth. The park hosts the most avian visitors, including the rare and majestic black-necked stork, in winter. In late spring and early summer all nature prepares for the coming of the monsoons, when the animals can rest from the eyes of the curious. These seasonal winds bring rain from the tropical oceans, and with them comes a renaissance. Roaring up the Bay of Bengal, gray, black, and purple clouds drop their wetness all along the south side of the Himalaya, watering the hills and plains of Nepal, Bangladesh, Bhutan, and India, and often flooding the parks. Asia's rivers are the second greatest source of water. In the Himalaya, or far beyond in Tibet, the world's highest plateau, rise Asia's mightiest rivers—the Yellow, Yangtze, Mekong, Salween, Ayeyarwady, Brahmaputra, Ganges, Sutlej, and Indus—waters that affect nearly half the world's population. I journeyed to the plateau, called the "Roof of the World," to see the upper reaches of these rivers and to learn more about a remarkable wildlife reserve.

Climbing from the plains of India, through Nepal, and crossing the Himalaya is an unforgettable adventure. You leave behind the jungles and humid climes of the mountains' south face, then wind up and up until you arrive at a 17,000-foot pass. Beyond it stretches the plateau, with its never ending vistas of brown, gray, yellow, russet, and beige undulations and its luminous, soft blue skies. Here on the other side of the Himalayan range lies a high desert where life of any sort seems painfully sparse. Then, suddenly, a marmot pops its head out of a burrow. A crowlike chough croaks from a crag.

Tibet has more than 500 species of birds, and the most dramatic in my eyes is the bearded vulture, or lammergeier. It materializes out of the sky like a roc from another eon on wings that span ten feet. This vulture is the only one of its family to have feathers on its head and neck, and thus represents a point between eagle and vulture—an eagle that lives on carrion and bones. Lammergeiers are champion fliers; one was seen flapping at 24,000 feet near Mount Everest. The bearded vultures soar on updrafts like hideous black gliders, racing along ridges to descend abruptly to the site of their next meal.

Far to the north of Tibet's main population centers near the Yarlung Tsangpo River, local name for the Brahmaputra on this side of the Himalaya, is the awe-inspiring and forbidding Chang Tang Reserve. It is home to an immense new nature preserve founded in 1993. Lying between 15,000 and 17,000 feet, the park is as large as the state of Arizona. It protects one of the world's last virgin zones, a harsh, treeless realm of constant winds, winter temperatures of minus 40°F, and little precipitation, yet where snow, rain, or hail are possible any day of the year.

Within these inhospitable conditions is an ecological zone that supports a rich and admirable fauna. Here roams the wild yak *(Poephagus grunniens)*, symbol of all that is free and powerful in Tibet. A full-grown male can weigh 2,000 pounds, has 30-inch-long horns, and runs with remarkable grace on dainty hoofs, its long, dark hair streaming in the wind. Once hugely abundant, the wild yak is reminiscent of the North American bison, its relative. Both have 14 pairs of ribs, are shaggy, have heavy shoulders, and groan rather than low. Its vocalizing, both whimsical and mournful, accounts for the yak's species name, *grunniens*, which means "groaning." Like the bison, the wild yak has been overhunted. Its numbers have reached a dangerous low throughout Tibet, and it has now retreated to this remote reserve. In the Aru basin region at the reserve's western edge roam the last herds of these proud animals; the largest holds perhaps a thousand individuals. The kiang, the Tibetan wild ass, is an elegant equine representative that roams the Tibetan expanses, living off the sparse grasses and scrub. When the kiang is startled, its long legs can carry it at speeds approaching 40 miles per hour. A herd racing along the horizon line looks like a swift, gray cloud, or a mirage in motion.

The Chang Tang's most spectacular display is the summer migration of the Tibetan antelope, when thousands of females and their young travel south from birthing grounds in as yet unknown sites in the Kunlun Mountains. At the beginning of this century a British observer in northern Tibet saw 15,000 to 20,000 of these timid, graceful antelopes at one time; today the numbers have diminished, and only four migrating groups are known on the Tibetan plateau. The herds have their freedom—for now—reflecting the essentially pristine state of the Chang Tang Reserve. Threats exist, though, for these and other precious animals of the wilds—Tibetan gazelle, blue sheep, argali, snow leopard, and Tibetan brown bear. Subsistence hunting among nomads has always been a tradition, but added to it today are commercial hunting and sport hunting. Both pursuits are completely illegal, yet are indulged in by officials. The greatest danger to the antelope is the demand for its soft and lustrous wool, which brings a fine price at its ultimate destination, the

Asia

looms of Kashmir. The growing materialism of Tibetans makes the risk and hardship of hunting and trapping antelopes worthwhile.

The potential for environmental catastrophe is far less here at the Chang Tang Reserve than in Nepal or India, and this fact raises major ethical and practical questions for conservationists. Should they put scarce resources at the disposal of regions that are in the direst condition? Can humans save some nearly extinct species? Or should protection come to a vast wilderness like the Chang Tang right now, though grave threats and devastations may not arrive for 30 more years?

One animal more than any other stands as a humble and dying witness to all the questions and problems raised above. George Schaller, the field biologist who throughout the 1980s studied and lived with giant pandas and fought for their survival, describes the panda as "a symbolic creature that represents our efforts to protect the environment…a species in which legend and reality merge, a mythic creature in the act of life."

The plight of the giant panda is well known. Only about a thousand of these animals exist, pushed into ever shrinking habitats beyond the eastern Himalaya in the border region of China and Tibet. The panda, adapted to survive solely on bamboo, is a specially evolved, perfectly adjusted being for its wet, montane environment. It has marvelous chewing teeth and special jaw muscles for crushing and stuffing its mouth with bamboo grasses; it can eat half its body weight each day.

Fate has been unkind to the panda. Nearly all remaining pandas live in the Wolong Natural Reserve and other sites in Sichuan Province. Sichuan, by far China's most populous region, contains 115 million people. If it were an independent country, it would be the world's eighth largest. Encroachment, habitat destruction, poaching, mismanagement, and other ills threaten the survival of the panda; Dr. Schaller entitled his most recent book *The Last Panda*. The greatest hope for pandas and for all endangered wildlife is to secure entire habitats and make them inviolable.

Kosi Tappu Wildlife Reserve, in contrast to famous Wolong and Chitwan, is a little-known gem in the far eastern corner of Nepal. Kosi Tappu is Asia's largest inland wetland, second in size only to the vast marshes of Iraq. It holds as great a variety of birds and mammals as Chitwan, but only 200 tourists per year visit. They come to witness the reserve's outstanding feature—Nepal's last community of wild water buffaloes, a herd that had diminished to a mere 60 animals in 1977 but has rebounded to more than 100 today. Even the obscure wetlands of Kosi Tappu have been altered by man. In the 1960s India built a dam across the Kosi River for irrigation and hydroelectric power. Today, *another* huge dam, the Upper Aran Dam Project, backed by the World Bank, is contemplated. It threatens the last few Ganges River dolphins, otters, fishing cats, and many bird species. In addition, India's leasing of Nepalese territory has allowed thousands of people from burgeoning Uttar Pradesh State to surge northward into the park region.

Two local naturalists from a rotating team of six are at Kosi Tappu at any one time, but they cannot hope to control the influx of Indian immigrants, who net and shoot birds, trap dolphins while catching the enormous eight-foot-long river catfish, and introduce grazing livestock.

Naturalists and zoologists interested in Asia's last pockets of wild buffaloes and other ungulates have been astonished by news from Vietnam in the past three years. The Vu Quang Nature Reserve in that country's border region with Laos, a lonely, ever wet world cut off from the rest of peninsular Southeast Asia, is extremely rich in biodiversity. It is home to the Asian elephant, gaur, tiger, leopard, Asiatic black bear, Malayan sun bear, white-cheeked gibbon, monkeys and macaques, many deer, and smaller mammals. In May 1992 a previously unknown species, the Vu Quang ox, joined this menagerie. The ox is a primitive member of the family that includes cattle, goats, and sheep. Scientists think the ox marks a point in evolution between cattle and antelopes. Only five new species of large mammals have been discovered this century, and if the treasure of the Vu Quang ox were not enough, another new mammal turned up in March 1994 in the same reserve! This is the giant muntjac (*Megamuntiacus vuquangensis*), a deer that joins its diminutive kin, the common muntjac. Responding to these remarkable finds, the Vietnamese government has increased significantly the size of the Vu Quang Reserve and is working to limit uncontrolled wood cutting and habitat clearance for agriculture within this unique zone.

Slumping leopard reflects the tragic dilemma of India's wildlife. After a poacher shot it, the wounded cat killed two villagers. Later immobilized, it heads for treatment. A soaring and impoverished population pressures Indian sanctuaries, competing with wildlife for scarce resources and stirring bloody encounters.

Farther still to the southeast, across the South China Sea on the island of Borneo, is Kinabalu Park, with 13,455-foot Mount Kinabalu as its centerpiece. The highest mountain between the Himalaya and New Guinea, Kinabalu is a granite wonder that rises through vegetation zones of dipterocarps, mountain oaks, rhododendrons, conifer forests, and alpine meadows to a summit realm of stunted bushes and grasses. I had always longed to see

Asia

this phenomenon of a great tropical mountain, but my main reason for coming was to find a python in the wild. The chances of such a meeting are small, but an ecologist friend who knows the jungles of Asia well said northern Borneo was a good place to attempt an encounter.

One evening under a large moon, with insect sounds filling the night air like a whirring motor, I crept along a damp, dirt trail, my footsteps muffled to near silence. Ahead of me to the right I saw a log, slightly curved and nearly 12 feet long. Something about it seemed odd, and then suddenly, as if a veil lifted, I saw moonlight reflected off ten thousand tiny scales and two glassy eyes. Here was my python!

Large constrictors—the boas and the pythons—are capable of moving swiftly when challenged or alarmed, but to my amazement this one held its ground and allowed me to approach. I sat down on the earth and stroked the sides of the snake with my two hands. The creature simply shuddered. It did not turn and attempt to bite me, but began a slow retreat into the black jungly undergrowth. For an instant I considered capturing the serpent—but how, and why?—and the thought of a hard struggle alone in the dark Borneo night dissuaded me. I positioned myself so it would slither across my legs, and that is what the glorious, illuminated reptile did—deliberately and steadily—until its slender, pointed tail disappeared into the gloom.

This experience more than any other affirmed for me the importance of preserving the creatures of the earth, of making safe forever parks and sanctuaries for all living things. We need nature's diversity for survival, for our food, and for our health. Beyond these practical reasons, we need animals to help us understand ourselves and to keep alive the mystery and wonder of our existence. My numinous python was a gift from the night, an emblem of Asia's wildlife riches—a talisman of all that is good and important.

Every extinction of an animal species diminishes each of us, and it damages our hope for the world. Loren Eisely, the great paleontologist and naturalist, lover of land and sea and the history of life, summed up an ancient ecological view of living with the earth and the animals, and stated a warning, too: "Do not forget your brethren, nor the green wood from which you sprang. To do so is to invite disaster…. One does not meet oneself until one catches the reflection from an eye other than human."

Sumatra

Poised for a sip, an orangutan, the sole great ape species of Asia, opts for a topsy-turvy splash in a Sumatran stream. The red apes, which once ranged throughout Southeast Asia, now survive in the wild only on Sumatra and the neighboring island of Borneo.

Malay Peninsula

Spreading "petals" among the blooms, a flower mantis of the Malay rain forest (below) presents a disguise fatal to visiting insects. A dead-leaf mantis (opposite, top) faces a threat with forelegs upraised. Other eye-catching denizens of the tropical rain forest of the Malay Peninsula include the five-spot moth, the black-spot tortoise beetle, and the dead-leaf grasshopper. "It was very dark and the insects were in full song, their symphony rising and falling, led by an unseen conductor," wrote naturalist G. Causey Whittow of a jungle hike in Taman Negara National Park. In tropical rain forest evolved over 130 million years dwells a trove of wildlife large and small, including elephants, tigers, rhinos, and 150,000 kinds of insects.

Borneo

Gravity powers the flying dragon (opposite). When it picks up enough speed, the lizard flattens out of its dive and glides to rest in a tree. It folds its "wings" and feeds on insects as it heads up a limb or trunk—then sets off again. Only on Borneo does the proboscis monkey dwell in the wild, and only the male sports the eponymous nose. Troops of huge males with harems of snub-nosed females half their size range watery forests in Sarawak's Samunsam Wildlife Sanctuary and along the Kinabatangan River in Sabah.

Asia

Chang Tang

Below bleak, furrowed hills of China's Chang Tang Reserve races a herd of kiangs, wild asses of Tibet. Established in 1993, the Chang Tang covers 115,500 square miles. Sacred abode of deities uncounted, the sere plateau rises three miles above sea level—hardscrabble home of the endemic Tibetan woolly hare (opposite), as well as grazers, predators, and the stock of nomadic herders.

Asia

Hokkaido

Beauty unbowed, a hardy pair braves a blizzard that shrouded their huddled flock of whooper swans, a species closely related

to America's trumpeter. Japan's cold northern island preserves generous swaths of wilderness and parkland, precious breathing room for wildlife and people in a crowded nation.

Siberia

Vast herds of reindeer—not quite wild, or captive either—roam Arctic wastes of Siberia. Herders, pursuing an ancient—yet changing—lifestyle, attend the reindeer wanderings, see to their health and safety, and in the fall dispatch some to winter range, others to butchers. For Siberian tigers, largest of cats, it has come to this: Captives, such as these in a zoo, outnumber wild ones by more than two to one. In southeastern Siberia, a sliver of their former range, scarcely 400 survive, preying on boar and elk, hunted by poachers while logging desolates their habitat. With captive breeding and research, scientists hope to preserve Siberian tigers in the wild.

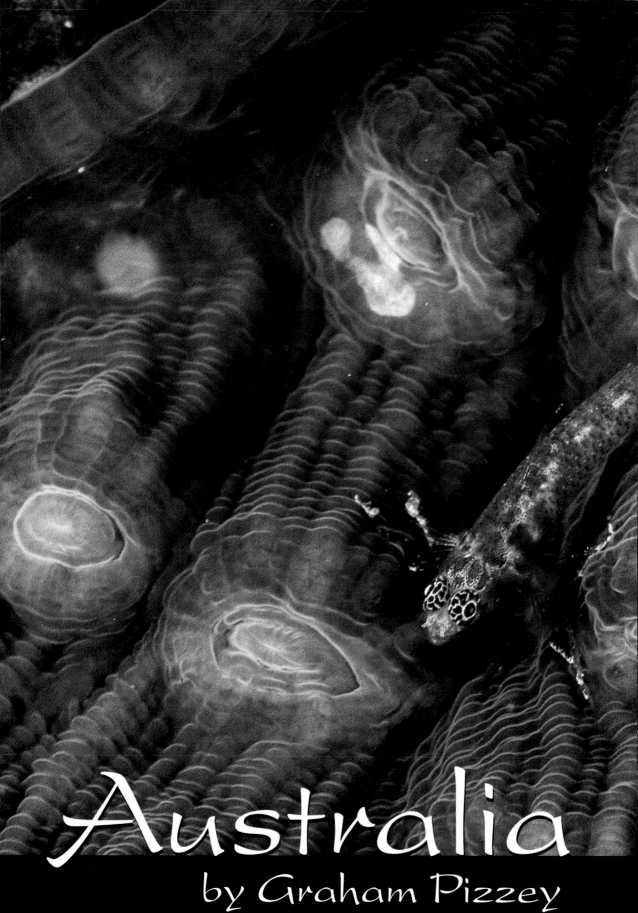

Australia
by Graham Pizzey

Neon bright, a triplefin blends with the coral glow of Australia's
Great Barrier Reef. Semitransparent skin also helps the fish hide safely.

AUSTRALIA IS UNLIKE any other continent. It is, in effect, an enormous ark, where plants and wildlife developed in isolation for millions of years. Australia's natural vegetation, its endemic mammals, birds, amphibians, reptiles, and insects are unique. It was only a few centuries ago that European explorers discovered this virgin continent of unbroken 50-million-year lineage. They found that Australia had living systems wholly new and different from any they knew.

In November 1845, German-born explorer Ludwig Leichhardt, on an epic 3,000-mile crossing of tropical northern Australia, found his intended route to the coast blocked by formidable sandstone escarpments. With no map, footsore, ragged, out of shot for securing game, Leichhardt recorded the vista from a hill he climbed to check the way: "I had a most disheartening, sickening view over a tremendously rocky country. A high land, composed of horizontal strata of sandstone, seemed to be literally

Moist and mossy, a high bluff in Queensland's Lamington National Park whispers with the splash of Morans Falls. Cascades in Australia are rare, confined mostly to the coastal uplands. Kangaroos range throughout the continent. A gray kangaroo joey hugs its mother, a prelude to pouch nursing.

Australia

hashed, leaving the remaining blocks in fantastic figures of every shape...."

Leichhardt did escape from this forbidding wilderness, and as his small party moved north across the coastal floodplains, those high-walled sandstone escarpments—with their gorges and fissures and vast tumbled blocks and boulders, along with rock shelters and fantastic Aboriginal art galleries yet to be discovered—slipped behind. People of several local Aboriginal clans welcomed the explorers warmly and guided them through a maze of freshwater wetlands to safety. Among them were the people now known as the Gagudju, after their language. The Gagudju—Kakadu is a European corruption of the word—were the successors to this astonishing land and its artistic legacy.

But all that was an age ago—in more ways than one. Since Leichhardt's day there have been fundamental changes. The sandstone escarpments and patches of tropical forest draining to the fissures and gorges he described in his journal are now part of Kakadu National Park. Each year some 250,000 visitors from across the world come to this great park created to protect the wildlife and its habitats, the rock galleries, and, one hopes, the way of life of the surviving Aboriginal people of the region.

Kakadu National Park lies in the tropics between latitudes 12 and 14, with its headquarters some 160 miles east along the Arnhem Highway from Darwin, capital city of Australia's Northern Territory. The park represents Australia's entire 50-million-year span of vegetational changes and fruitful coevolution between plants and wildlife. Created in stages by the Australian Parliament between 1979 and 1987, at more than 7,600 square miles Kakadu is one of the largest and richest national parks on earth. Nearly the size of Wales, larger than New Jersey, twice as large as Yellowstone, it is by any measure a generous representation of wild Australia. Wealthy in every natural dimension, Kakadu has some 1,000 species of plants, 280 of birds, 60 of mammals, 60 of fish, 75 of reptiles, more than 25 of frogs, and an estimated 10,000 of insects.

Topographically complete, with a 56-mile tidal, mangrove-fringed coastline on Van Diemen Gulf, the park embraces the drainages of four rivers: the Wildman and the East, South, and West Alligator Rivers, named in 1820 by the naval explorer Philip Parker King after their many saltwater crocodiles, *Crocodylus porosus*, which he mistook for alligators.

How did Kakadu get so rich? How were the great sandstone escarpments formed? Where did the diverse communities of plants and wildlife come from? The very antiquity of human occupation here is mind-stretching—yet human beings were among the last living things to arrive. To begin with, the hard, residual sandstone of the escarpments in Kakadu are part of the Arnhem Land Plateau, a landform estimated to be some 1.6 billion years old. The escarpments were here more than a billion years before the first animals with backbones arose, and far before the world's present continents took shape.

Laid down over old volcanic rocks, sands carried in by some great river system built up over time to depths of three miles or more.

Australia

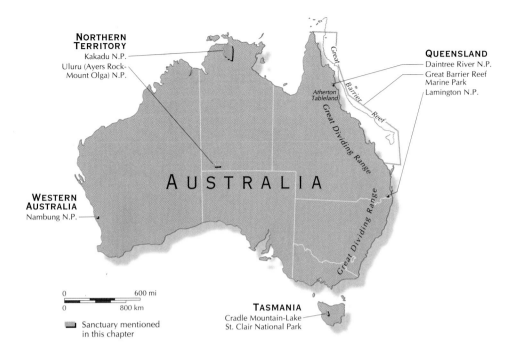

NORTHERN TERRITORY
Kakadu N.P.
Uluru (Ayers Rock-Mount Olga) N.P.

WESTERN AUSTRALIA
Nambung N.P.

AUSTRALIA

QUEENSLAND
Daintree River N.P.
Great Barrier Reef Marine Park
Lamington N.P.

Atherton Tableland

Great Barrier Reef

Great Dividing Range

Great Dividing Range

0   600 mi
0   800 km

Sanctuary mentioned in this chapter

TASMANIA
Cradle Mountain-Lake St. Clair National Park

Compressed and heated by their own weight, the sands consolidated to form the hard Kombolgie Sandstone, the basic formation of today's Arnhem Land. Overflowed in parts by lava from subsequent eruptions, over an ocean of time the plateau has been faulted, fissured, carved by wind and sand and rain, but its western escarpment still soars 800 to 1,000 feet above sea level. For a time, in the Mesozoic, it became a series of sea cliffs, eroded by waves; but still it stands, its warm, buff-colored walls and ramparts extending as far as sight carries. Although roughly only 1,500 feet high, these fractured, beetling sandstone walls look majestic because they wind over 300 miles through Kakadu, are often viewed from below, and are garlanded with galleries of vivid green monsoon forest. After the wet season in Australia's summer, many high waterfalls thunder down their gorges. It is spectacular country.

Between 50 million and 40 million years ago, Australia was born as an isolated continent when it separated from the far-southern landmass, Gondwana, and began a long, lonely drift north toward Asia. Clothed in cool rain forests and palm swamps, it carried a Noah's ark of ancestral Australian wildlife: early marsupials, egg-laying mammals like echidnas and platypuses; parrots and cockatoos, many waterbirds, even songbirds; also amphibians, reptiles, freshwater fish, and insects.

As the continent moved north away from the moisture-circulating winds of the Southern Ocean, increasing heat and aridity began to roll back the original rain forests. Remnants survived mostly on the lowlands and highlands of coastal eastern Australia. The now much-reduced but still fabulous patches of rain forest in regions like Atherton Tableland in tropical northeastern Australia still reflect *(Continued on page 120)*

Australia

Sanctuaries of
Northern Australia

Daggerlike teeth punctuate the saltwater crocodile's reputation as the most feared of its family. Brisk commercial demand for the crocodile's tough hide puts the reptile's survival at risk. A great number of its kind find safe haven in Kakadu National Park. Fair game for the crocodile, a double-wattled cassowary takes a daring river bath. Shy, the bird prefers thick forests, fending off obstructions in the underbrush with its bony forehead helmet. Also a woodland dweller, the red-eyed tree frog hangs out in Australia's damp coastal forests.
FOLLOWING PAGES: A jabiru, Australia's only species of stork, primps in Kakadu National Park, a major refuge for many kinds of tropical birds.

F*ur with a sheen of lime qualifies the green ringtail possum (opposite) as one of nature's rarest mammals. Unlike nest-building possums, this species curls up in a tight ball and sleeps in the open on a tree limb. Its fur camouflages it among the leaves and moss on branches, and divided central nails on its front feet help it climb. The green ringtail lives only in Queensland rain forests, where it subsists solely on the leaves of fig trees. Ficus trees lack commercial timber value; hence they survive even when an area is logged. A spiny anteater, or echidna, bristles with spiked fur. Its strong foreclaws tear open ant beds and termite mounds. Its barrel snout gives deadly aim to a sticky tongue that can quickly lap up the routed insects. FOLLOWING PAGES: Microscopic claws on the underside of its toes pin a leaf-tailed gecko to a tree in Daintree River National Park, a rain forest in northeastern Australia.*

Australia

the glory of the Gondwanan forests and still contain many of their plant families and even genera.

Because soils in the tropical northeast are volcanic and comparatively rich in nutrients, rainfall and humidity levels high, and elevations greater, the forests are taller, cooler, damper, denser than those in Kakadu. Among the grandest trees are broad-barreled kauri pines, genus *Agathis*, a group of conifers of Gondwanan origin widely represented on southern continents. Elkhorn ferns and orchids grow high in their moss-padded limbs, which also support huge, looping water vines. As might be expected, these luxuriant, ancient rain forests support a splendid diversity of wildlife. There is the cassowary, a large, shaggy bird that pushes through undergrowth with a hornlike helmet. There are several bowerbirds, one of which, the golden, makes the largest display bowers known. There is a close relative of the birds of paradise, the Victoria riflebird, which displays spectacularly in shafts of sunlight. Among mammals, amid a cohort of possums, there is a beautiful green ringtail, while kangaroos are represented by the tiny rat kangaroo. A very curious offshoot of this large hopping fraternity is Lumholz's tree kangaroo, which tried to reverse evolution by returning to the trees. Here, too, are the amethystine python, one of the world's biggest snakes; some handsome tree-climbing dragon lizards; and the Cairns birdwing, one of the world's largest butterflies.

Over much of the rest of the continent, millions of years of aridity, high temperatures, and nutrient-deficient soils have drastically changed the original, rich rain forest habitats. Australia is now the world's driest continent: More than half has a median annual rainfall of less than 12 inches; nearly a third has less than 8 inches. In contrast, some coastal areas receive more than 13 *feet* of rain annually. A band of green grazing lands, croplands, woodlands, and forests occupies the southeastern corner of Australia in a satellite view and extends north along the coast on both sides of the Great Dividing Range to the tropical northeastern tip.

Extensive, seasonally wet, fertile tropical pockets rim the north-central coast (where Kakadu lies), and a well-

*W*ith upright stance, foldout collar, and nasty hiss, a frilled lizard uses scare tactics to bluff hungry enemies.

watered, cool-temperate pocket lies in the southwest, around Perth. Much of the rest of Australia, especially the vast interior, is arid, with spectacular ranges of hard, red-black, ancient sandstone, and, west of center, oceanlike deserts of rolling, east-west dunes of oxblood-colored sands. Uluru, our great, far-inland national park of more than 500 square miles, with its celebrated monolith Ayers Rock, epitomizes the region.

Though these lands are far from being conventional deserts, 100,000 or more feral camels, descendants of draft animals imported from Egypt and Arabia last century, and introduced European rabbits, foxes, feral goats, and horses are doing their damnedest to make them so. Twenty million years of adaptation in these arid interior regions have produced plants able to withstand heat and desiccation and to respond quickly after rain, producing seeds and copious blossoms attractive to finches and to pollinating birds such as wood swallows and honeyeaters. They, in turn, are able to breed quickly at almost any time of year in response to rain.

In August–September 1993, I traveled west from Alice Springs through those deserts after a winter of good rains. I saw endless soft sage greens of new foliage against red sand, all touched with the gold and pink and white of many blossoms—of eremophilas (desert lovers), mulla mullas, grevilleas, and several species of eucalyptus, such as the ghost gum, which has developed snow-white trunks to reduce the effect of heat and solar radiation. Stretching far between these flowering sandhills rolled swales and seas of orderly hummocks of porcupine grass, *Triodia*, which grows in doughnut-shaped rings, three to ten feet across. All had tall seed stems, and the desert breeze furrowed and tossed these waist-deep, bronzed seed heads like crops of wheat. Flocks of seed-eating green budgerigars chattered out of the grasslands as I passed, or congregated at water holes to drink. I passed alert, crested spinifex pigeons and stately Australian bustards striding softly in search of small reptiles and rodents, whose tracks in the sand were numerous. Some desert!

Along the north coast, and in what is now Kakadu, the changing conditions of climate that produced arid conditions inland made rain forest survival less certain. Today's patches of monsoon rain forest, in their dense coastal form and in pockets in the sandstone escarpments, had to shift and colonize as they could. Less mighty and luxuriant than the original rain forests represented on Atherton Tableland, these monsoon forests, which become drier in the winter dry season, are nonetheless a very important component in the Kakadu tapestry, even if they occupy less space than the eucalyptus woodlands and grasslands. With their emergent, endemic Carpentaria palms, Kakadu's coastal monsoon rain forests are inhabited by birds such as fruit pigeons and orioles in the high canopy, flycatchers in the middle levels, and rainbow pittas on the leaf-padded forest floor, where orange-footed scrub fowls scrape up vast incubator mounds.

The isolated patches and gorge-filling belts of monsoon rain forest on the sandstone escarpments hold a distinct and varied range of plant species, mostly descended from original far-southern families. A large,

Australia

lively, green flowering tree of these picturesque gorges, *Allosyncarpia ternata*, first described in 1976 and still with no common name, was valued by local Aborigines. They sheltered under it, ate honey made from its flowers by small native bees, used its wood to make fighting sticks, and stripped bark from its trunk to heal sores. Fig trees of several species, with their astonishing ability to drive their rubberlike roots into every crevice for moisture and nutrients, cling to precipitous rock faces and provide fruit and resting and nesting places for birds such as banded fruit pigeons. The endemic white-lined honeyeater's brisk, lively call reverberates through all these forest pockets, while the voice of the sandstone shrike-thrush, a deep, mellow cadence ringing and echoing, seems the very soul of the escarpments. There are many medium to small terrestrial and arboreal mammals here: insect-eating bats and fruit bats ("flying foxes," which form enormous seasonal "camps" and are a favorite food among Aborigines). There is an impressive range of reptiles, from 12-foot Oenpelli pythons to venomous death adders, dragon lizards to legless lizards.

In contrast to these monsoon rain forests, Kakadu's gray-green eucalyptus woodlands, which cover a much greater portion of the park, are more open and sunny. They include some splendid flowering trees, among them the orange-blossomed Darwin woollybut and the swamp bloodwood, with its large, deep pink blooms. Colored to attract pollinating birds, these blossoms flow with nectar, energy food for lorikeets (nectar-eating parrots) and honeyeaters—two of Australia's most widespread and characteristic bird families. With an understory of acacias, grevilleas, banksias, and pandanus trees, this eucalyptus-dominated plant community represents the tougher and thriftier vegetation that developed to replace the wilting rain forests as the Australian continent grew hotter and drier.

You cannot travel far in Kakadu's woodlands without hearing the rolling, rusty trumpeting of red-tailed black cockatoos. Going to water on the plains at dusk, they fly with strange, buoyant, floating beats of their long, black wings, displaying brilliant scarlet or lemon tail panels and bugling news of their arrival. In the shrubby understory of the eucalyptus woodlands, sounds of bird mimicry, coupled with deep swearing and hissing, often signal that a great bowerbird is performing. Building a double avenue of incurving twigs and grasses on the ground, it decorates a platform at one end of this avenue with huge collections of bleached bones and shells. By selecting display objects of the same tonings and reflectiveness as the bill and plumage of rival males and by seizing the objects and displaying manic vigor and aggression, the male bowerbird attracts potential mates and warns off rivals. At least, that's one theory concerning bowerbird behavior.

Meanwhile, in the blue overhead, black kites wheel, and green and peacock blue rainbow bee-eaters soar and dash after dragonflies and bees.

The mammals of these forests include the primitive, egg-laying spiny anteater, or echidna (a large cousin, now extinct, is present in rocky art galleries). There are leaf- and nectar-eating possums and a whole suite of wallabies. Indeed, the wooded escarpments have produced some charming variations on the kangaroo theme—tiny, almost catlike rock wallabies, which bounce from rock face to boulder like rubber balls, and black wallaroos, sturdy, rock-haunting kangaroos whose fur color matches the weathered sandstone. There is a cohort of eager-faced marsupial hunters, from the size of a tiny mouse to that of a cat, and (formerly) a large, marsupial "wolf," the thylacine (now extinct), whose portrait was painted thousands of years ago on a rock face. The thylacine was probably driven to extinction by the arrival 4,000 years ago (in the canoes of later Aborigines) of an Asian dog, the dingo, now the top terrestrial predator in Kakadu apart from man. In even earlier prehistoric times, the fauna also included giant, plant-eating wombats the size of hippos.

The woodlands shelter northern Australia's celebrated frilled lizard, which mostly emerges in hot weather. Large ones grow to a length of nearly three feet. Spectacularly colored reddish, yellowish, and black, the lizard is famed for its enormous erectile neck frill. When confronted, this reptile rises on its hind legs, hissing and swaying, and spreads its frill. The show is all bluff, however. When it can, it turns and hurries away on its hind legs, frill neatly folded, and takes refuge by climbing a tree.

Linked with the sunny, open eucalyptus woodlands are Kakadu's great grasslands, which run through the wooded foothills and sweep far across the coastal floodplains. They represent a later stage of plant development, when aridity and fire cut swaths through the woodlands, allowing the spread of fast-growing annuals such as grasses. Their success led to a proliferation of grazing and browsing animals, dominated by species like today's agile wallabies and larger antelopian wallaroos. Abundant, and mostly of a size a man could spear and carry, kangaroos and wallabies became an integral part of Aboriginal life and lore.

Padded with dense, spiny hummocks of porcupine grass, *Triodia*, the sandstone escarpments provide habitat for an endemic grass-wren and a native rock pigeon. So tied to these ancient habitats are these two birds that their plumage patterns repeat either the sharp *Triodia* blades or the granular roughness of the rocks and their red and black shadows. The lowland grasslands also sheltered some impressive birds important to Aborigines for food—and for drama: the huge, flightless emu; one of the world's heaviest flying birds, the Australian bustard; and the brolga, Australia's big crane, whose courtship "dances" the Aborigines adopted. A handsome company of grass finches, including the Gouldian finch, feed on the seeds of native grasses. Farther out on the plains, immense migratory flocks of little curlews, as well as plovers, pratincoles, and other shorebirds, fly almost nonstop from breeding grounds in Arctic Siberia to spend the southern summer in the endless grasslands and wetland fringes of northern Australia.

Although Kakadu represents Australia's ancient past, it can claim to be biologically "modern." That is because, about 6–8,000 years ago,

Australia

following the close of the last Pleistocene ice age, some fundamental changes occurred that had a profound local influence.

As polar ice caps melted, world sea levels rose. Weather patterns changed, and climates grew more humid. In the Kakadu region, the coastline advanced some 185 miles inland. The present monsoonal climate of intensely wet summers was set in place and gave birth to the great freshwater wetlands, with their staggering populations of waterbirds, crocodiles, and fish. In this, the driest continent, it is unusual to see waterfowl in great concentrations. In Kakadu, I have seen 100,000 magpie geese feeding on *Eleocharis* corms. The multitude stretched far into the heat haze, and so many other birds—herons, egrets, jacanas, glossy ibis, storks, darters—were present that any meaningful count of numbers was impossible. I gazed in awe, immersed in the subdued roar and fluty gabbling and honking, the upending and digging.

The extra dimension of higher summer rainfall, coupled with the proximity of marine life as the sea encroached up the rivers, put an even richer gloss of abundance and diversity on what was already there, to the benefit of the Aboriginal inhabitants, who are estimated by some to have been in the Kakadu region for perhaps 50,000 years. Under the new seasonal conditions and especially after freshwater wetlands replaced salt marsh on the floodplains about 1,500 years ago, yams, corms of spike-rush, stems of water lily and giant red lotus, edible fruits of rain forest trees, "cabbage" from palm shoots, and leaves, fruits, and berries from monsoon forest trees were all to be had in season. There were kangaroos and wallabies; geese and goose eggs; estuarine fish such as sawfish and barramundi; mussels; and file snakes, pythons, and crocodiles.

It seemed that everything needed for a rich life was present in Kakadu. There were trees for making dugout canoes, weapons, implements, and music sticks, and plants that provided cords, netting, dyes, ceremonial paints, and containers. The Aborigines were well prepared to profit from the new fertility. But the golden age was not to last forever.

On one of his last mornings in what is now Kakadu, Leichhardt calculated that there were 200 Aborigines at his camp. Based on his reports, the local Aboriginal population has been estimated at perhaps 2,000. Following Leichhardt, almost everything Europeans did, benevolent or hostile, seemed in the end to affect Aborigines adversely. The Gagudju people declined from approximately several thousand in 1845 to fewer than one hundred by the 1970s. Their traditional living areas lay bereft of caring, educated owners. They had known every water hole, camping place, and food source. Their lives were part of a natural tapestry.

As a respected Gagudju elder, Big Bill Neidjie, said a few years ago: "People they can't listen for us. They just listen for money....Our story is in the land....It is written in those sacred places....This story is important. It won't change, it is the law. It is like this earth, it won't move."

Given this fundamental wisdom, it is ironic that the rise of uranium mining in northern Australia from the 1950s on, coupled with a growing national awareness of a desperate need to act on Aboriginal health and land rights, led to the regrouping of a scattered and demoralized Aboriginal people under terms more favorable than they could ever have conceived. This turn of events came about partly because, among all its other wealth, Kakadu is also rich in uranium, gold, platinum, and palladium. Several of its uranium deposits are regarded as among the richest on earth.

In the 1970s, under pressure from miners, conservationists, and Aborigines, the Australian government decided to call a wide-ranging public inquiry into Aboriginal land rights and uranium mining in the Northern Territory. As a result of that inquiry, provision was made for two mines as well as a national park. To meet the aspirations and help secure the future of the Aboriginal people, title to large areas of land was granted to the scattered traditional Aboriginal owners, who had formed a body called the Gagudju Association to represent their interests. The creation of Kakadu National Park was seen as a means of protecting and managing their newly won land in a way compatible with their traditional way of life. To ensure secure management, they leased the land back to the Australian National Parks and Wildlife Service, now the Australian Nature Conservation Agency. For the first time in more than a century, the Aborigines could see a glimmer of hope of reestablishing their traditional life. As we approach the year 2000, one mine—the Ranger—remains. For the moment, it is the only uranium mine operating in Kakadu, and its deposits are being worked out. With its ancillary buildings, treatment plant, and tailings dam, it lies within an enclave in the national park. The nearby town of Jabiru, population now about 1,500, houses mining staff, government employees, and Aboriginal people who wished to move there.

Decimated by all the debilitating influences that accompanied European colonization, but again growing, Kakadu's Aboriginal population is the direct successor to 50,000 years of human life and all the artistic inheritance that legacy embraces. The rock paintings in Kakadu, which span 20,000 years of human occupation, are ancient enough to portray animals now extinct, yet modern enough in their later stages to capture European sailing ships and horses. The oldest paintings in these Aboriginal galleries are thought to predate those at Altamira in Spain and Lascaux in France. Today there are more than 5,000 individual rock-shelter galleries, some more than 130 feet long and crowded with images.

Collectively, these countless thousands of paintings, from early hand silhouettes to highly developed X-ray style representations of fish, turtles, crocodiles, kangaroos, other game animals, and people, represent a pinnacle of human culture. One of the world's great art collections, it is also a condensation of wild Australia in its ancient glory.

The galleried sandstone escarpments, monsoon forests, and eucalyptus woodlands of Kakadu, the pillared rain forests of tropical northeastern Australia, and the vast interior of red sandstone and desert dunes still sustain communities of plants and animals unique to that ancient ark—a continent gloriously different from any other.

Australia

Tasmania

Soaring headwalls of fluted stone frame snowcapped Mount Geryon and a mesalike formation named the Acropolis. This stark view unfolds atop Cradle Mountain in one of the last true wilderness areas on earth, Cradle Mountain–Lake St. Clair National Park in Tasmania. Forests of the refuge protect some of the world's oldest and most exclusive species; they include the eastern quoll (above, right), the legendary Tasmanian devil (opposite), and other marsupials isolated by the breakup of Gondwana 50 million years ago.

Australia

Great Barrier Reef

In tight formation, sweetlips glide above a coral garden off the northeastern coast of Queensland. A series of reefs, stretching like a tiered underwater veranda through these tropical waters, form the Great Barrier Reef. At least 350 different coral species have built the labyrinth. Spread across more square miles than England and Scotland, the reef provides food and shelter for countless marine creatures. Beaked leatherjackets (above) dart around antler coral branches to dine on small crustaceans and coral polyps. A spider crab (above, right) hunts on an arm of gorgonian coral.

Uluru

Armored with sharp barbs, a thorny devil tops a dune in Uluru National Park. This native of Australia's desert interior resembles North America's horned toad, and like its cousin eats ants by the thousand.
Another Uluru resident, the seldom-seen marsupial mole, needs no eyes or external ears. It spends most of its life underground tunneling with shovel-like claws in search of insects and insect larvae to eat.

Nambung (Overleaf) ▷

Pillars like tombstones bearing scars of time and erosion rise above wind-rippled sands in the Pinnacles region of Nambung National Park. Australia, a continent unlike any other, preserves flora and fauna that are also unique.

Australia

Fur flies as a bobcat snatches a snowshoe hare in Colorado's White
River National Forest—one of North America's oldest timber reserves.

North America

by Kenneth Brower

THE KING OF MAMMOTH gathers his harem in the evenings on the lawn of the Mammoth Hot Springs Hotel. The lawn is a magical commons. It is ambiguous turf, one of those rare and unlikely intersections of the natural and the unnatural worlds. The kings of Mammoth, as the locals call the dominant bull elk of this region of northern Yellowstone National Park, have for generations made good use of the lay of the lawn. Highway 89 to the east, the hills to the west, the barrier of the hotel to the south, and the century-old barracks of Fort Yellowstone scattered conveniently, all help the bulls keep their cows and calves herded up. The reigning bull of 1994 had assembled, by mid-September, a harem of between 30 and 40 cows. It was the bull's first year of primacy.

My son was asleep in the back seat when we arrived at Mammoth. I parked so that the bull, standing in profile on the lawn, entirely filled the

Colorado's quaking aspens flag autumn in Uncompahgre National Forest. In northern Montana a gray wolf bares sharp fangs. Of all North American wildlife, this hunter ranks as the top big-game predator, but centuries of slaughter wiped out wolf populations in some areas.

North America

ARCTIC CIRCLE

UNITED STATES (ALASKA)
Arctic N.W.R.
Kodiak N.W.R.
Denali N.P. and Preserve
Wrangell-St. Elias N.P. and Preserve
Tongass N.F.
Glacier Bay N.P. and Preserve

CANADA
Kluane National
Park Reserve
Jasper N.P.
Riding Mountain N.P.

Hudson Bay
Cape
Churchill

UNITED STATES
Flathead N.F.
Gallatin N.F.
Yellowstone N.P.
Grand Teton N.P.
Bridger-Teton N.F.
Gray Lodge State Wildlife Area
Yosemite N.P.
White River N.F.
Uncompahgre N.F.
Los Padres N.F.
Chiricahua N.M.
Everglades N.P.

NORTH
AMERICA

0   1000 mi
0   1500 km

Sanctuary mentioned
in this chapter

BELIZE

COSTA RICA
Monteverde Cloud Forest Reserve

view out my windshield. The span of his antlers was enormous, with six
points on either horn. The hair of his chin looked wet and slavery and
slicked back. His lower belly and the dark ruff of hair there pumped
spasmodically, as if in prelude to marking. His eyes were insane, all
cataract-cloudy with testosterone and sleeplessness and combat and lust.
There came a distant bugling of another bull, across the state line in
Montana. The bull on the lawn hearkened. Raising his chin, he dropped
his antlers back close to his spine and bugled an answer. Again the
challenge from Montana. Again this Wyoming bull answered. The evening
air filled with the wild, lovely, strangled trumpeting of bull elk in rut.

I reached back for my son's leg and gently shook it. David is eight
and not a heavy sleeper. His head came up slowly, and he glanced out the
windshield. Never have I seen him cross so quickly from sleep to
wakefulness. His eyes got big before he was conscious. "Dang!" he said.

The elk, on cue, lowered his head and waggled his antlers, tearing
up a section of turf with the points. He urinated, marking the grass
beneath him, then commenced a subtle sort of hula, imparting a circular,

North America

lawn-sprinkler motion to the stream. It splashed against his back legs, then came around to splash them several times more. For good measure he shot the stream straight forward into his chest, then dropped his chin between his forelegs to anoint that too, and finally lay down in the musky bed of pheromones and pee he had made for himself. *"Dang!"* my son said again, two-thirds admiration, one-third disgust.

A day later, walking some miles south in the autumnal vastness of the valley of Gardners Hole, David and I saw white motes drifting at the far side of Swan Lake. The lake's namesakes, I guessed, as I brought out binoculars. No other bird in Yellowstone, save the white pelican, is so large and so bright. Magnified ten times, the motes became, indeed, a pair of trumpeter swans. The trumpeter, *Cygnus buccinator,* is the biggest swan in North America, and it has the loudest and deepest voice. This pair, multiplied by their reflections, made four swans upon the lake. The four white necks were long and elegant, the four beaks completely black. One bird left the other and glided across the stillness. The moving trumpeter was a little jiggly, for ten-power binoculars are hard to tame completely, yet somehow the tremor only accentuated the smoothness of its passage. The swan was paced by its own dazzling image. Its wake made a thin line of chaos through the reflected autumn of the hillside beyond.

West of Swan Lake, in a valley at the southern end of the Gallatin Range, we walked through the woods to stretch our legs at dusk. On the branch of a dead aspen at the edge of the fir forest—awaiting nightfall—perched a great gray owl. This species, one of the biggest owls in North America, is a bird of the far north. It is rare this far south. This one had no fear of us, refusing to fly even when we approached to within ten feet and stood under its branch. Over the bird's shoulder was Electric Peak, named for its attraction to lightning, but the evening was cloudless, the peak uncharged, and for now the only electricity was in the yellow, night-piercing eyes of the owl. The owl looked down on my son, swiveling, bobbing, and weaving owlishly to see and hear him from various angles. The two struck up a conversation, the owl answering each of David's imitation hoots with the genuine cry of an owl.

"In a world older and more complete than ours," naturalist Henry Beston wrote in 1928, "they move finished and complete, gifted with extensions of the senses we have lost *(Continued on page 147)*

Sanctuaries of Greater Yellowstone

FOLLOWING PAGES: A bull elk bugles in an early snowfall in Yellowstone National Park. Alive with elk, grizzlies, bighorn, and bison, some 14 million acres of hot springs, mountains, fields, and forests referred to as Greater Yellowstone include several wilderness preserves and two national parks.

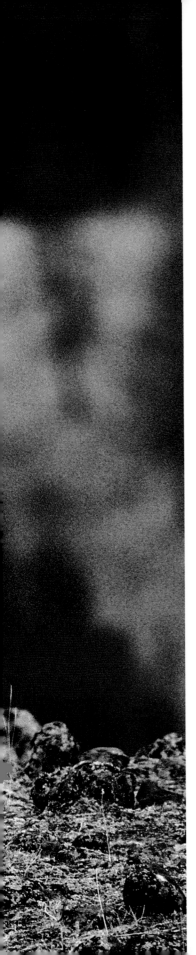

*On the trail of food, a grizzly follows its sensitive
nose, sniffing from smell to smell. The bear enjoys meat,
but vegetation—grasses, roots, and berries—forms the
mainstay of its diet. Plants also offer material
for resting, bedding, and denning. Human activity has
devastated the bear's habitat; only about 200 grizzlies
remain in Greater Yellowstone. A program to help
restore the bear population guarantees six million acres
of prime grizzly habitat free from human hassle.
The curled upper lip of a bighorn ram signals
the prelude to mating during the autumn breeding
season in Yellowstone National Park.*

North America

*W*isps *of steam rise as bison cows and calves ford Yellowstone's Firehole River; nearby thermal springs heat the Firehole. Unlike the bison, the coyote has extended its range despite human encroachment. A jackknife pounce brings one its next meal. The Tetons (opposite) loom more than 12,000 feet in the namesake park near Yellowstone's southern boundary. FOLLOWING PAGES: Wintry solitude wraps a mountain lion stalking in the rimrock and timbered slopes of Montana's Gallatin National Forest, which borders the northern edge of Yellowstone National Park.*

or never attained, living by voices we shall never hear. They are not brethren, they are not underlings; they are other nations, caught with ourselves in the net of life and time, fellow prisoners of the splendor and travail of the earth."

I was happy my son had encountered, on this aspen branch, the other nation of the great gray owl.

On still another day, we sat in the grass of Hayden Valley, at the center of the park, watching a herd of bison graze. Hayden Valley is an old arm of Lake Yellowstone, dried up, and the lake in its turn is a vestige, cooled down, of the great caldera formed by an ancient cycle of volcanic eruptions at the center of the park. The autumn grass of the valley was lion colored. The tawny hills to either side were black with pines along the crests. Beyond the dusty shuffle, the tail whisking, the grass chomping, the minor altercations, and the basso buffo grunts of the near bison grazed a small herd of farther bison, dark humps in the golden grass, and beyond that herd were the specks of herds more distant still. This was the other nation of the bison. Indeed, the Lakota Sioux, anticipating Henry Beston, called them Pte Oyate, Buffalo Nation. Migrating across the sky, not much faster than the Buffalo Nation across earth, was a procession of stately white September cumuli. This was a scene from Catlin, or Moran, or some other old prairie painter. It felt like racial memory, though I must have borrowed it, I supposed, from some other race. My son is part Indian. Perhaps the memory was his, and I was just eavesdropping.

A raven flapped overhead and landed nearby. Davey, more interested always in near animals than far, forgot all about the bison. He addressed the raven in uncanny raven-talk he learned somewhere—a voice I have never been able to duplicate. With the first concussive wing beats of the arriving raven, with that shiny, perfect blackness of feathers, that wicked eye and Roman beak, it seemed that the whole landscape jumped a little, as if the last piece of a puzzle had fallen into place. In the mythology of many Northwestern tribes, Raven is the trickster-creator. That original bird, *Corvus corax*, had arrived, and this picture was now complete.

"The first step in intelligent tinkering is to save all the parts," wrote the naturalist Aldo Leopold. Here in Yellowstone, saved both by intelligence and by happy accident, are all the parts.

"I seek acquaintance with Nature,—to know her moods and manners," Henry David Thoreau wrote in his journal. "Primitive nature is the most interesting to me. I take infinite pains to know all the phenomena of spring, for instance, thinking that I have here the entire poem, and then, to my chagrin, I learn that it is but an imperfect copy that I possess and have read, that my ancestors have torn out many of the first leaves and grandest passages, and mutilated it in many places."

The elk is one of those grand passages. So are the trumpeter swan, the bison, the great gray owl. In the book that Thoreau borrowed from his natural library in Concord, Massachusetts, the elk, swan, and bison had been ripped out, but here in Yellowstone those pages are intact and unsmudged. The pronghorn antelope, fastest terrestrial animal in North America, and the grizzly bear, largest land carnivore on earth, and the moose, the giant deer that makes even the elk look small, all range freely here. The grand passages of cougar, bighorn sheep, golden eagle, and white pelican are all still legible. One important page—the wolf—has been missing. An erratum slip for *Canis lupus* was prepared by the Park Service. Recently, several pairs of wolves have been slipped back into the volume, with apologies. Yellowstone, if not quite an entire heaven and an entire earth, is a good piece of both.

Yellowstone is an idea as much as a stretch of terrain. The great sanctuary, first national park in North America, is a vision, a template, a seed; and it spread. In the realm the biogeographers call the Nearctic, which combines North America and its great satellite Greenland, there are now more than 2,000 official parks and sanctuaries, with an area of more than a million square miles. None of the seven other realms of the earth—not the Afrotropical, Indomalayan, Australian, Oceanian, Antarctic, Palaearctic, or Neotropical—has protected so much. Of the 22 biogeographical provinces in the Nearctic, all but one, the Greenland Tundra, are represented in parks—and that frigid province has the de facto protection of its remoteness and interminable winters. The Rocky Mountain Biogeographical Province has more than 200 reserves protecting about 50,000 square miles in the Nearctic. One of the largest of those reserves—and at 3,500 square miles the biggest national park in the lower 48—is Yellowstone.

Yellowstone is the mother of parks, but certain of its offspring now dwarf it. Wrangell-St. Elias National Park and Preserve, in Alaska, at more than 20,000 square miles—nearly six times the area of Yellowstone—is by far the largest park in the United States. Its contiguous counterpart, Kluane National Park Reserve in Canada, protects about 8,500 square miles. Wrangell-St. Elias/Kluane makes a gigantic international sanctuary. At the eastern end of the Nearctic, Greenland National Park, at more than 375,000 square miles, is by far the biggest park on earth.

It has been my good fortune to spend a good part of my career wandering Nearctic parks. The bargain has been Faustian. I have had to pay for every moment of freedom in the wilderness with long periods of confinement in small rooms behind a typewriter, but I believe I would do it all over again. In Yosemite National Park I saw my first black bears. In a five-week walk across the Arctic National Wildlife Refuge, at the age of 22, I saw my first barren ground grizzlies, Dall sheep, and barren ground caribou. (When the caribou are in migration, earth trembles, and the whole landscape seems to flow away vertiginously. With the decimation of the bison, the caribou make our last great herds. The Arctic tundra has become our final North American Serengeti.) In Jasper National Park, in Alberta, and Riding Mountain National Park, in

Manitoba, I followed moose and elk and mountain goats. On the outer coast of Glacier Bay National Park and Preserve, in southeast Alaska, I saw my first and only wolverine. On kayak trips through the straits and sounds of Tongass National Forest, in Alaska, I had the company of Steller's sea lions, ringed seals, sea otters, bald eagles, humpback and killer whales. From the summit of Mount Pinos in Los Padres National Forest, I watched the last wild California condors sail by on nine-foot wingspans.

If I learned anything in these travels, it is that big animals need big spaces, and that habitat, for wildlife, is everything.

Nothing has brought these lessons home better, I think, than the condor. In the 1980s I wrote several articles on the controversy over the fate of that bird. The California condor, *Gymnogyps californianus*, is the supervulture of North America, a great soarer, its wingspread wider than that of any other North American land bird. By the early 1980s the condor, its numbers reduced to just 19, had become one of the continent's most endangered species. Environmentalists and ornithologists were divided into two camps, one for capture and captive breeding of the entire wild population of condors, the other for letting the condors alone. I tried to be objective, but I found myself falling in with the latter faction.

It became increasingly clear to me, in contemplating condors, that this species—any species—is an interaction between DNA and a particular place. Remove a species from its place, and it becomes a different animal. In a narrow legal sense, the removal is a mistake, for if you take an endangered species—spotted owl or condor—out of its habitat, then the habitat loses its statutory protection. The removal is fatal in a larger, Darwinian sense, too.

The great wings of the condor were shaped by the dry hills that form the thermal updrafts upon which those wings were meant to ride. A condor reared in a cage, without that buoyant pressure underneath, is an imitation condor. And condorhood is not a simple business. Each condor must learn, from its elders and from experience, where to find food and where to nest, how to compete with golden eagles in the air and with other condors on corpses. It must master countless other small tricks and details of condor life about which we are ignorant. All that learning is tied to a particular terrain and a particular piece of sky. Sanctuaries are not simply important to wild animals; they *are* the animals.

This account has focused, so far, on big creatures, the "grand passages" in that book of Thoreau's. But there are shorter passages, too, in the natural history of North America. After the grand passage of the wolf comes the more modest passage of the coyote. The meek—or the undersized at least—sometimes really do inherit the earth, and the coyote now rambles most of the realm formerly ruled by its larger cousin. It was a coyote—*Canis latrans*—that my son and I saw mousing in the meadows of Yellowstone, not *Canis lupus*. After the grand passages of the great gray owl and the great horned owl, posing their deep, Solomonic questions, come the shorter queries of the screech, long-eared, and saw-whet owls.

North America

After the grand passage of the trumpeter swan, there is the fine declarative sentence of the water ouzel, or American dipper. David and I, on our way to observe bison, were delayed for two hours one morning by ouzels in the Yellowstone River. Since early childhood, the ouzel has been a favorite of mine. It is a bird for all seasons, as happy in snow as in sun, and does not bother with winter migration. The ouzel is a bird for all mediums. It is as happy walking the bottoms of fast streams as hopping and dipping on streamside boulders, as happy flying underwater as flying through air. Never before had I watched ouzels through optics as powerful as those I possessed that day in Yellowstone: my new ten-power binoculars and the unjaded, eight-year-old eyes of my son. We noted how the plumage of the ouzel, sooty gray in air, turns silvery with bubbles when the bird flies underwater. We noticed how the last of the stream to spill from an ouzel is often a smoothly polished, uncut diamond of icy water between the shoulder blades. We wondered at the ceaseless, joyous hunting of ouzels. We laughed at all the energy an ouzel expends when it is putatively at rest: the endless preening, fluffing, oiling, stretching, and wing calisthenics necessary to keep cold-water gear in working order.

In the talus piles above the ouzel streams there is the short, exclamatory, oft-repeated sentence of the pika, barking its piping bark from atop its castles of rock. There is the overpunctuated sentence of the porcupine. There is the acrid sentence of the skunk.

There is the epigram of the ant. The ant, after the grand passages of moose and elk and bison, might seem insignificant, but the ants of North America have more biomass than all the moose, elk, and bison combined. One day in Yellowstone, on our way to watch bighorn sheep, we were delayed for ten minutes in observation of a big, black worker ant sharing my son's ham sandwich. Removing my glasses, I held the sandwich up to my eye—myopia and myrmecology go together nicely— and I made a close monocular study of the lavish sculpture of the wasplike waist and, on the segment just anterior, the bladelike spine on the petiole protecting that narrow isthmus of the ant. I discerned the white, nearly microscopic hairs on the abdomen. I quailed a little before the onslaught of the huge, implacable, serrate jaws butchering ham. The ant, from this vantage, was as awesome as any grizzly.

In the end, though, it was the unequivocally big animals that drew Davey and me. Big animals are the measure of our great sanctuaries, and the reason for them. Ants, sanctuaries or not, will survive us and whatever insults we heap on the ozone layer and our forests and rivers and seas.

We returned again and again to watch buffalo, and we came to know the lines of *Bison bison* well—the bluff, nearly vertical faces of the bulls; the more gradually sloping, more typically bovine faces of the cows; the tasseled fly whisk of the tail; the insulated forward end of the animal, woolly leggings on the forequarters, woolly cape on the hump, with dreadlocks of bison fleece sometimes hanging—a chic, unwashed, Rastafarian look. The bison is clearly a creature designed for facing into winter. The hindquarters, when compared to the front end of the buffalo, appear lean and disproportionately small. Each bison seems to have been overtaken by some smaller, faster prairie ungulate that has telescoped into it from behind.

To me, the hump, the horns, the mammoth-like wool of the cape all whispered "Pleistocene." They whispered "megafauna." Bison have been in Yellowstone since the end of the Pleistocene epoch. They are survivors of the outsized fauna preserved in the La Brea tars. The bison of the North American Pleistocene knew mastodons, tapirs, and giant ground sloths. They ranged with camels and horses, two creatures that originated on this continent. They ran from giant dire wolves, *Canis dirus*, and from atrocious cats, *Felis atrox*, and from the genus named, with wicked irony, *Smilodon*, the saber-toothed cats. In death their bones were picked over by the enormous short-faced bear, *Tremarctotherium*, and by the giant condor, *Teratornis*, and by the somewhat smaller condor *Gymnogyps*, another survivor—barely—of that old time.

The insect, reptile, and bird faunas of North America were not as diverse as those of the claustrophobic rain forests of South America. This continent offered, instead, open vistas, big mammals, great herds. North America's sanctuaries protect a remnant of that colossal age. For sheer ursine size and power, the short-faced bear has its analogue in the huge grizzlies of Kodiak National Wildlife Refuge. The giant ruminants of the Pleistocene have worthy successors in the enormous moose of Wrangell-St. Elias and Kluane. The howl of the dire wolf—if that huge, fearsome wolf did howl— is echoed today by the wolves of Denali. The rumble of the great herds still resounds in the caribou sanctuaries of the Alaskan and Canadian Arctic.

The Yellowstone idea has not simply scattered to the wind, like thistle gone to seed. The idea has grown in place. Ecologists today are less interested in Yellowstone than in what they call the Greater Yellowstone Ecosystem. The sanctuaries that form this system—among them Yellowstone and Grand Teton National Parks at the center; Bridger-Teton, Caribou, Beaverhead, Targhee, Shoshone, Gallatin, and Custer National Forests; Gros Ventre, Fitzpatrick, Bridger, Washakie, Teton, and Absaroka-Beartooth Wildernesses; North Absaroka Wilderness Area; Red Rock Lakes National Wildlife Refuge; and the National Elk Refuge—were faits accomplis before anyone quite realized that they made a whole. Their connection was less a discovery by humans than by bears. Radio collars on Yellowstone's grizzlies showed that they wandered well beyond the borders of the park. Their home was Greater Yellowstone, not lesser. Following this grizzly hint, humans are beginning to manage Greater Yellowstone as one *ecos*, one "house."

The growth of the Yellowstone idea has not stopped at the borders of Greater Yellowstone, either. Of late, ecologists and environmentalists, poring over their maps again, have seen that corridors joining Greater Yellowstone, Greater Salmon, Greater Glacier/Continental Divide, Greater Hells Canyon/Wallowa, and Greater Cabinet/Yaak/Selkirk would

North America

unify the Northern Rockies bioregion. In 1993, to that end, the Northern Rockies Ecosystem Protection Act was introduced in Congress. Should it pass, Greater Yellowstone and its satellites will become rooms of a single, and still greater, house.

The idea has not stopped there. Conservation biologists and biodiversity activists based in Oregon have begun what they call the Wildlands Project. By a system of core reserves, corridors, buffers, and restoration zones, these visionaries propose to heal and reconnect wild ecosystems and landscapes all across North America. "Our vision is simple," reads their mission statement. "We live for the day when Grizzlies in Chihuahua have an unbroken connection to Grizzlies in Alaska; when Gray Wolf populations are continuous from New Mexico to Greenland…when humans dwell with respect, harmony, and affection for the land; when we come to live no longer as strangers and aliens on this continent." This notion is, of course, wildly wishful. It is quixotic, a pipe dream, just whistling in the dark. It is simply a new step in the old ghost dance by which the Plains Indians of the 1890s, half-mad with hunger and loss, hoped to conjure back the buffalo.

But what a fine dance it is! There are worse dreams in circulation. Better the ghost dance than some new craze like the leveraged buyout.

One afternoon in Yellowstone, David and I stopped for a herd of bison crossing the road. As the buffalo left the asphalt, we watched a bull following a cow, his nose to her tail, in the dull, plodding way of amorous male bison. Suddenly the bull tired of this old pursuit. Letting the cow wander on, he threw himself down on a patch of bare hillside. There was a great explosion of dust, and all we could see in the cloud was the bull's legs in the air, kicking ecstatically. It is good to be alive, apparently, if one is a bison. Existence must seem especially sweet when your kind has been to the edge of extinction. Most of the bison alive today are descended from just 77 animals, which survived in five small herds. Pte Oyate, the Buffalo Nation, has returned from the very brink. Today Greater Yellowstone is a bison factory, with overflow animals spreading to lands beyond. Greater Yellowstone is an elk factory as well, and may soon be a factory for wolves.

In intelligent tinkering one saves all the parts. For a grand reconstruction along the lines proposed by the Wildlands Project, all the necessary parts are on hand. Yes, that dream is a ghost dance. But in its own time Yellowstone, the original national park, was a ghost dance, too. It was magical thinking that worked.

Chiricahua

Head-on encounter reveals the dark patches and large head that distinguish the black-tailed rattler, one of many reptiles that thrive in Arizona's 17-square-mile Chiricahua National Monument.

North America

Cape Churchill

Nose-to-toes calisthenics entertain a polar bear cub in the frozen far north
of Cape Churchill, on the western edge of Hudson Bay.
Games and exercise such as this help build the cub's agility and stamina
in preparation for long treks to the sea, when it tags along with its mother
in search of food. Polar bears prey mainly on seals.
The arctic fox shadows the bears onto pack ice, feeding on scraps from their kills.
In spring, the foxes feed on rodents, birds, and fish.
Unlike polar bears, which retain their white fur all year,
arctic foxes turn brown in summer.

Everglades

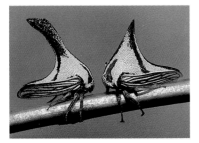

Out for a stretch in the sun, a diamondback rattlesnake winds across a mangrove (below) in Florida's Everglades National Park. A subtropical river wilderness of mangroves, saw grass, and palm-tufted hammocks, the Everglades fills a saucer-shaped depression a hundred miles wide that reaches from Lake Okeechobee to Florida Bay. Within the park living wonders flourish: snakes and snails, alligators and fish, and a variety of birds; it remains among the last Florida breeding grounds of the roseate spoonbill, which cranks its head from side to side as it looks for frogs, fish, and insects in the marshy shallows. In recent years

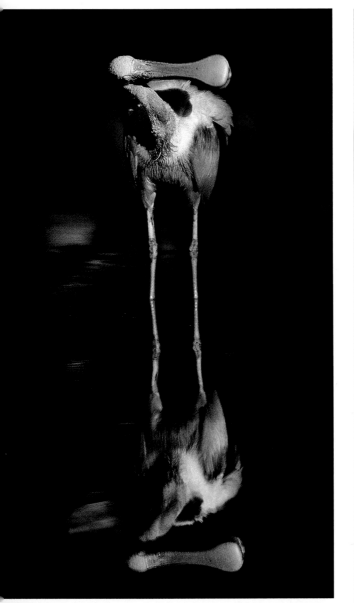

the spoonbill has increased in numbers in southern Florida.
Thorn bugs pin their security
on large sail-shaped spines designed to discourage hungry birds.

Gray Lodge (Overleaf) ▷

Beating wings churn the air at sunrise above Butte Sink in California's
Gray Lodge State Wildlife Area. The wetland draws flocks of Canada geese and
other migrating waterfowl to the sanctuary near Sacramento.
No other single state shelters the huge numbers of wintering waterfowl
that California does. In Gray Lodge and the surrounding Sacramento Valley,
more than a million birds may take flight in one day.

Central America's
Tropical Forests

Delicate tracery mirrors its background as a translucent frog clings to leaves near a stream in the Monteverde Cloud Forest Reserve of Costa Rica. Its skin, nearly as transparent as a window pane, earned the 2-inch-long amphibian its nickname—"glass frog." Tropical forests of Central America house a rich variety of wildlife. Strongest and largest cat in the Americas, the jaguar (right) strides across a forest floor in Belize. At night the graceful feline hunts capybaras and otters. The jaguar still abounds in the unspoiled wilds of Belize, but it has nearly disappeared from many Central American haunts. European settlers, who staked out ranches in the late 1800s, killed the cats to protect their herds, and hunters shot the animals for their hides. Also common in the forests of Belize, the jaguarundi (below, right) slinks along river edges in search of birds and small mammals.

Denali

Above timberline, a grizzly waddles across subarctic tundra in Alaska's Denali National Park, the nation's premier bear country. No other U.S. sanctuary guards a more visible and diverse community of wildlife. In early spring, a herd of some 4,000 caribou races across the park. The hoofed nomads sometimes pause, munching lichens and other plants like commuters on the run as they migrate to summer pastures in the Alaska Range.

North America

Flathead

Golden eyes gleaming, a gray wolf in Montana's Flathead National Forest gauges its next move. Elusive by nature, wolves have decreased in number due to hunting by ranchers. A snowy owl, seemingly snug in frostbite weather, depends on its layered plumage for more than warmth. Soft, comblike wing feathers deaden the sound of the bird in flight, allowing it to swoop down on unsuspecting prey. The snowy owl breeds mainly in Arctic regions, but when food grows scarce this keen hunter heads south, putting in rare appearances at such U.S. reserves as Montana's Flathead.
FOLLOWING PAGES: A Canadian lynx, one of North America's most secretive cats, pads past Flathead timber. The forest marks its southern range.

North America

Protected from human predations but not from natural ones, a young marine iguana succumbs to a hawk in Galápagos National Park.

South America

by Tom Melham

SOUTH AMERICA'S WILDLIFE IS LEGEND. Ever since the conquistadores started sending back phantasmagorical accounts of the strange and wondrous creatures here— of headless men and female warrior societies and, yes, cities of gold—the world has learned to *expect* the unusual from this fantasyland-come-true.

Its startlingly diverse biology made South America—not Africa or Asia—the continent of choice for Alexander von Humboldt and Charles Darwin, for Alfred Russel Wallace, Henry Bates, Richard Spruce, and other naturalists of the 19th century. These men were drawn to South America's wild coasts, to its mountains and islands, but mostly to its vast, jungled heart. "This uproar of life," Bates called the Amazon, where he collected nearly 15,000 different species, more than half new to science. In his day, South America was the least known, most fascinating continent a biologist could experience. To many modern biologists, it still is.

Home of the world's largest tropical rain forest (opposite), South America also harbors the greatest biodiversity. Its wildlife varies from Amazonia's stupendously colorful frogs and birds to the bellowing elephant seals (above) of Argentina's Valdés Peninsula.

South America

COLOMBIA
Puracé N.P.

ECUADOR
Galápagos Islands

VENEZUELA
Hato Piñero
Canaima N.P.

Orinoco Basin

EQUATOR

A M A Z O N

B A S I N

SOUTH
AMERICA

PERU
Manú Biosphere Reserve
Tambopata Reserve

*A
N
D
E
S*

BRAZIL
Pantanal N.P.
Das Emas N.P.
Poço das Antas Reserve

0   1000 mi
0   1500 km

Sanctuary mentioned
in this chapter

*A
N
D
E
S*

*P
a
t
a
g
o
n
i
a*

Valdés Peninsula
ARGENTINA
Perito Moreno N.P.
Los Glaciares N.P.
Tierra Del Fuego N.P.

CHILE
Torres del Paine N.P.

For although it harbors relatively few large mammals, South America boasts an enormous gallery of other creatures, some majestic, some weird, some downright scary. This, after all, is the realm of the jaguar and condor, of 30-foot-long snakes, spiders as big as your hand, and the most diverse collection of crocodilians anywhere. It is home also to the world's largest eagle, smallest deer, and biggest rodent. It is a land of myriad monkeys and brightly hued frogs, where eels come electrified and camels are humpless, where ants approach the size of mice. Earth's only marine lizard and its only aquatic marsupial live here, as do giant turtles, giant otters, and even more gigantic tortoises. Gorgeous, almost infinitely varied arrays of butterflies and birds flit through the forests.

While no taxonomist can say exactly how many species now share this planet with us, chances are good that more occur here than on any other continent. Of known species, South America has the most birds, insects, amphibians, reptiles, fish, and plants. A single square mile of eastern Ecuador, for example, can contain 80 types of frogs—about as many as inhabit all of the U.S. and Canada! South America boasts the world's biggest and most diverse rain forest, awesome both in size and in the wealth of life it supports. It has the mightiest waterway, the driest desert, and the longest continuous mountain chain; climates along its 5,000-mile length range from tropical to near-Antarctic. Its mix of high plains, sprawling wetlands, brutally spectacular coasts, and oddball island groups all help make this continent one of the richest fonts in the animal kingdom. And yet, wrenching changes increasingly threaten its wildlife bounty. South America is no longer a sparsely populated paradise. Its ballooning human population is transforming even once remote regions. While the continent claims more than 700 national parks and reserves, enforcement of their regulations often exists more on paper than in reality. Duke University veteran research biologist John Terborgh, with over 30 years of field experience in the Amazon basin, is deeply concerned.

"Nearly the entire Amazon," he told me over coffee in Cuzco, Peru, "has been shot out, emptied of its large mammal fauna. It's been absolutely decimated, on a scale you're not prepared to imagine. All across Brazil and Venezuela, Colombia and Bolivia, everywhere. There are very, very few places where the fauna is intact."

One outstanding Amazonian remnant consists of the watershed of the relatively tiny Manú River, in southeastern Peru. Remote, bounded on one side by the steep eastern face of the Andes, on the other by nearly impassable rivers and jungle, the Manú drainage eluded Western man until an adventurous rubber baron stumbled upon it near the turn of the last century. While he and his tappers shot some of Manú's animals, they did far more damage to resident Indians, whom they deemed troublesome and soon annihilated. Several years later they departed, leaving Manú virtually unpeopled; its wildlife returned to levels that biologists feel are as rich as any in South America.

In 1973, thanks to dedicated conservationists and a dictatorship intent on boosting nationalistic pride, the Manú drainage became a national park. By coincidence, John Terborgh arrived that month. "I saw wildlife at a level of abundance that I'd never encountered anywhere else," he recalls. "And still haven't."

Christof Schenck, a Frankfurt biologist who has intensively studied Manú's giant otter populations, agrees: "It's a virgin area. You have a whole drainage as a national park, one of the biggest national parks on earth. And it's a hot spot of biodiversity."

Indeed, Manú may have more species than any other conserved area on earth. With elevations that plunge from nearly 14,000 feet above sea level to only 1,200, Manú's habitats run the gamut from *puna*—a cold, dry, tussocky version of alpine tundra—through elfin and cloud forests, to classic lowland rain forest. Other South American reserves either never possessed such diversity or lost it as civilization encroached.

Officially known as Manú Biosphere Reserve, Peru's premier wildlife refuge occupies some 7,300 square miles, an area nearly as big as New Jersey. Both its size and its proposed degree of protection make Manú unusual among South American reserves. John Terborgh especially praises what he calls its "passive defense": By including the Manú River's entire watershed, park designers ensured that the only practicable entry would be the river. Position a single guard station at that river's mouth, and you essentially control access *(Continued on page 181)*

South America

Sanctuaries of
Upper Amazonia

*"This uproar of life," naturalist Henry Bates called the Amazon basin;
life roars on even today in remnant areas of virgin forest, such as Peru's Manú
Biosphere Reserve, where red-backed poison dart frogs (below), capuchin monkeys
(top, right), and brightly banded grasshoppers (bottom, right) all thrive.
FOLLOWING PAGES: Manú also shelters the world's largest
concentration of giant otters, which feed on the area's plentiful fish.*

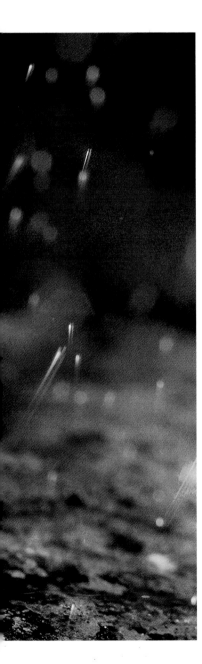

South America

Skinhead of the rain forest,
a white uakari lives in a small and
often flooded region of the upper
Amazon, rarely descending from
forest canopy. The uakari's
arboreal lifestyle helps it evade
the jaguar (above), too heavy for the
branches that support the uakari.
In Manú, not only the cats wear spots:
Vivid colors of Pachylis *bugs*
warn away predators.
FOLLOWING PAGE: A scarlet
macaw bursts from a riverside clay lick
in Tambopata Reserve, near Manú.

South America

to all New Jersey. The preserve's watershed-based boundary makes ecological sense as well, since wildlife hews to topographic rather than political barriers. Rugged terrain also helps protect the park. Though the dirt road from Cuzco spans only 150 miles, it's so snaky and steep that your truck or bus will take a day and a half to make the trip. And *then* you must transfer yourself and your gear to outboard-powered canoes that go down one river and then up the Manú, expending another full day reaching your destination.

Five hours' worth of switchbacks begin soon out of Cuzco, climbing up and across the dry, angular Andean highlands. Ridge after ridge passes—until you cross a final divide and find yourself at the lip of the Amazon basin. Some 13,000 vertical feet down the jagged wall of this enormous punch bowl lies the Manú River. Don't expect to see it, however, for the westward-moving trade winds pile up moisture-laden air along the eastern wall of the Andes, forming thick clouds and fog. What you *do* see is a totally different world from the sere puna you've just left: the elfin forest. Suddenly, trees! They may be scrubby and short and grayish green, but compared to the tawny, treeless puna, they're downright lush. Lichens cake their trunks and branches. No Andean snows water them, nor is rainfall significant; almost all moisture here is in the form of cloud and mists. Tanagers and hummingbirds zip by, reminders that this stunted forest supports 90-odd species of breeding birds—*twice* the number you'll find in any single habitat in North America, says John Terborgh.

The switchbacks, descending now, grow perceptibly wetter and greener; trees loom a bit taller, while lichens give way to mosses. Welcome to the cloud forest. Dozens of varieties of ferns, ranging from dainty to ponderous, scale sheer rock walls. Lacy bamboo garlands—slender, curved, punctuated with delicate bursts of leaves at each node—lend an Asian feel. Luxuriant trees jut out from near-vertical scarps. Begonias boast leaves two feet wide. Fifteen-foot-tall tree ferns seem throwbacks to Carboniferous times. Still no rain, yet waterfalls trickle and plunge. Mosses encrust forest branches with a secondary bark, layered in turn by bromeliads, fungi, orchids, and other growths.

With patience and a little luck in this primeval hideaway, you can see woolly monkeys, tiger-herons, woodcreepers, cinnamon flycatchers, various hummingbirds, perhaps an Andean solitaire. Blue-crowned motmots shift their bizarre, pendulum-like tail feathers back and forth. Scan a seemingly bare rock face carefully and you might find a nightjar boldly staring out from its perch, nearly invisible thanks to its rocklike coloration.

At the opposite end of the visibility spectrum stands the cock-of-the-rock. Arrayed in can't-miss orange-scarlet, males boast a feathery crest that resembles a Roman legionnaire's helmet. Early mornings and late afternoons, they gather at specific courting sites called leks. I spent several hours at one, a perfectly ordinary-looking tree that was very special to at least eight different males. Each chose a territorial perch, uttered an initial cry of *errrack*, and began popping its beak much as some humans crack

South America

their knuckles. Then all rustled their wings, made several head-ducks, and clucked out a steady, henlike *cock-cock-cock-cock-cock*. Suddenly, they fell silent for five or ten seconds, as if waiting for applause, before repeating their repertoire, sometimes from an alternate branch. A few drab females watched, apparently unimpressed.

Down in Manú's lowland forest, macaws and other parrots congregate even more densely—not at *leks* but at clay *licks*, not to seek mates, but rather to eat dirt. Researchers feel they do so to supplement their diet with certain minerals, some of which may help counteract the natural toxins found in many fruits and seeds they eat. Licks often occur along rivers, where moving waters carve the tawny clay into steep cutbanks that rise 20 or 30 feet high. Topped by mature trees, such banks can run for miles. Each lick, however, occupies only a few yards of bank. Just why parrots prefer one stretch of seemingly identical clay wall to another remains their secret.

Up before dawn one day, I join zoologist Charles Munn of the Wildlife Conservation Society in a thatch-covered canoe that serves as a floating blind, moored near a key lick. The eerie wail of howler monkeys alternately builds and ebbs, sounding at times like an approaching hurricane, at other times like a pulsing steam locomotive. Minutes pass, slowly. Somewhere above, mild chatterings signal to Charlie the presence of blue-headed parrots. Two scarlet macaws splash the treetops with red, blue, and yellow as they sound their distinctive, raucous call. More time passes, but the lick remains empty.

"This is the most dangerous thing they do," whispers Charlie, explaining that a lick's exposed surface poses double jeopardy for avian visitors: Ocelots may lurk on the nearby forest floor, while harpy eagles soar above. We wait some more.

Slowly, slowly, the blue-headed parrots descend a few at a time, hopscotching to lower and lower branches, waiting for their numbers to build to some unknown quorum before making the final plunge. Then a rush of wings; up to 80 birds jam the lick's narrow, five-foot-long ledge with a mass of green bodies, blue heads, and red undertails. Some nibble. Others yank out great gobs of dirt, clamping them in one clawed foot and devouring them as eagerly as children down snow cones in summer. Suddenly the parrots explode back into the trees, leaving the lick bare. We don't see what spooked them, but they refuse to return to that lick all day. Scarlet macaws later leapfrog down through the trees just as the parrots had—each species seems to have its preferred window of opportunity at the lick—but they, too, hold back.

Near another lick along a tiny side stream, fresh prints pock the damp river sand—the delicate spoor of peccary; a deer's cloven-hoofed imprint; the big, three-toed signature of a tapir; then the huge, unmistakable pawprint of what locals call *el tigre* (in Spanish) or *otorongo* (in Quechua, the language of the Inca). We know it as jaguar, among the most feared and shy of rain forest residents. On three previous trips into

Amazonia I had not seen a single jaguar sign and had nearly begun to doubt their existence. No longer.

The streambed also harbors some curious earthen dikes, perfectly circular, only a few inches high and a foot in diameter. Each holds a pool of water dotted with black bits of protoplasm: frog eggs and tadpoles. It is late August, Manú's driest time of year, and had the parent frogs not built these dikes, their eggs by now would have succumbed to dehydration or some aquatic predator. Soon the wet season will raise rivers, breaching these dams and allowing the emergent generation to disperse.

Soon I, too, head downstream—with local Machiguenga Indians in a small canoe powered by a *peque-peque*, their onomatopoeic name for the little four-cycle engines they use to navigate the often shallow, muddy, and snag-ridden Manú. Varied riverine habitats support a celebration of bird life. We see in quick succession white-necked herons and tiny white-winged swallows, colorful Orinoco geese, Muscovy ducks, a swallow-tailed kite. Roseate spoonbills and wood storks rare in Manú patrol the shallows. An osprey flaps ponderously. The effusive, lyrical song of an oropendola—a type of oriole—bursts out like the sound of bubbling waters. Terns and black skimmers rise from beachside rookeries to dive-bomb our passing canoe. Amazon kingfishers—smaller than North American ones, touched with iridescent green—accompany us, while toucans and red-and-green macaws perch high in canopy trees. So much to see here, all so open to view. Experiencing Manú is a privilege.

For days my main goal in the park has been Cocha Cashu, one of several *cochas*, or oxbow lakes, spawned by the meandering Manú. Cashu—named for its nutlike shape—harbors the research station where John Terborgh has done his fieldwork for the past 20-odd years. I've been told that a student biologist, Pepe Tello, is there and might guide me through the lowland forest. The Machiguenga boatmen pole and power our canoe through countless bends in the river; rounding yet another curve, we spot a lone figure, waving. Could this be Pepe? Indeed it is. His waving, however, is less a welcoming gesture than it is an attempt to flag a ride. For Pepe must go to Lima, *pronto*. He gives his two-minute camp tour—here's the john, the water pump, the lab, a crude map, the radio, and frequencies to monitor. Here's the generator, but, sorry, it's out of oil. Have to go now, *adios*. And he and the boatmen depart. I am alone in the jungle. As I begin ferrying my gear and food the half a mile from riverside to the station on Cashu's shore, a vulture alights in the small tree nearest me. Is this an omen? Maybe he just caught a whiff of my rations, which include a dried joint of llama.

That night, brilliant stars poking through tiny gaps in the forest canopy make me eager to see more. I push off from shore in a dugout canoe and silently glide out into the treeless expanse of Cocha Cashu, eyes on the sky's incredibly star-smitten dome. Suddenly the water behind me erupts in a gigantic splash; my flashlight reveals two red, glowing eyes nearly as big as tennis balls. A resident black caiman apparently wants me to know I am not really alone. Comforting thought. The species grows up to 20 feet long, and while it usually prefers fish to human flesh, I don't want to be a test case. I find myself concentrating less on the stellar display overhead, more on keeping the tippy dugout on an even keel.

By day, Cashu seems anything but threatening. Lizards skitter noisily over dry leaves. Hoatzins—spiky-headed, blue-faced birds that look like punk-rock chickens—huff and puff from shoreside branches. Black spider monkeys bound unhesitatingly through mature forest, nimbly leaping from branch to branch without ever descending to ground level. Sturdy prehensile tails—a Neotropical invention—give them the advantage of a fifth hand. I watch a mother bridge one void in the canopy with her own body, clinging to branches front and rear while her youngster grapples across, using her fur for handholds. Both see me yet remain relaxed. In many other places in Amazonia, both spider and woolly monkeys are much more shy, for they are favorite foods of local Indians.

These and 11 other primates live in or near Manú, ranging in size from 20-pound red howlers to tiny tamarins; biologists have estimated that they represent 40 percent of the area's mammalian biomass. Not a day passes that I don't manage to spot at least three different species. Once, I don't even have to get out of bed. That's the day monkeys descend on the research station like Visigoths sacking ancient Rome. Branches begin to sway, then thrash. Scores of furry bodies rapidly materialize, swinging and springing from tree to tree, ripping foliage for fruits and insects and other good things to eat. It's a mixed troop: Capuchins—both brown and white-fronted—and lots of smaller and even noisier squirrel monkeys, along with some species of marmoset. A steady rain of ravaged seed pods, flowers, leaves, half-nibbled palm nuts, and other debris rattles down as this conquering army lingers nearly an hour about the station, foraging on the fat of the understory. Then, as abruptly as it began, the monkey barrage is over, its storm troopers gone to greener pastures.

Manú's forests—even its highest and driest ones—contain thousands of different plant species. Yet this lushness and variety arise from soils that are almost invariably poor, continually leached of minerals by frequent rains and ever growing vegetation. How is it that earth's richest gardens stem from some of its poorest soils? Because life in the rain forest is lived ever on the brink. Year-round warmth means no fallow time, no seasonal slowdown as occurs in temperate forests. Without that slowdown, leaves and other debris do not accumulate into thick humus, but are dismantled and recycled into living tissue almost as soon as they hit the forest floor. Here more than anywhere else on the planet, we see the ephemeral nature of nature. Life is not a gift, merely a loan. Tropical forests function on a higher metabolic plane than temperate ones. Thus their intensely competitive, richly varied plant life—and their chronically depleted soils.

Similarly, notes otter biologist Christof Schenck, the oxbow lakes "have very low nutrient levels—but they have very many species of fish, perhaps a hundred." Just as the forest immediately turns its detritus into more greenery, the cochas quickly transform their debris into more fish.

The fish in turn support important populations of predators such as black caimans and giant otters—locally known as *lobos del rio* (river wolves). Highly visible and once common throughout tropical South America, both species suffered dramatic declines due to heavy hunting. Now protected, otters approach 6 feet in length and 70 pounds in weight. They are gregarious and territorial. A family of eight patrolled Cocha Cashu when I was there. Despite murky, low-visibility waters, frequent squeals and chompings attested to their success as fishermen. Each adult, says Schenck, needs ten pounds of fish a day; Terborgh estimates that the average otter family consumes more than 30,000 fish yearly! While these sleek and engaging predators may claim several lakes in their territory, their appetites and length of stay here underscore the richness of small Cashu.

Habitats, of course, determine wildlife. Take the mesa-like *tepuis* of southeastern Venezuela. Arthur Conan Doyle immortalized these flat-topped, sheer-sided, rain-forested mountains as "The Lost World," a realm so isolated that he imagined dinosaurs had survived there into modern times. While no velociraptors roam the tepuis today, other biological relics do. Strange frogs barely larger than a thumbnail, which cannot hop but rather crawl, are one of this area's highly endemic species, protected along with the forest and savanna of Canaima National Park.

Another remote "lost world" of wildlife consists of Argentina's Valdés Peninsula. This treeless near-island midway between Buenos Aires and the Straits of Magellan is known for great aggregations of elephant seals and sea lions, seabirds—including jackass penguins—and whales. Terrestrial residents include rheas and roadrunner-like tinamous. Farther south lies the stark beauty of Patagonia, home to pumas, guanacos, and bird life that varies from condors to cormorants, from ducklike sheldgeese to flamingos and ibis. Patagonia's prime refuges are Chile's Torres del Paine and Argentina's Tierra del Fuego, both national parks.

Colombia's Puracé National Park provides a high, humid haven for some of the continent's oddest and shiest mammals: Spectacled bear, mountain tapir, and the Andean pudu—the world's smallest deer, little more than a foot tall. Another park, Das Emas in southern Brazil, offers gallery forests and savannas rich in termite mounds, anteaters, tapirs, capybaras and coatimundis, and nearly a hundred bird species.

Brazil, the continent's largest and richest nation, also claims spectacular wildlife—as well as a long history of emphasizing development over preservation, and of poorly enforcing what conservation measures it enacts. Its unique populations of golden lion tamarins, for example, have dwindled to fewer than 600 animals, despite the creation of Poço das Antas Reserve near Rio de Janiero. One of this country's most impressive wildlife jewels remains the vast wetland of the Pantanal. John Terborgh

South America

considers it "an absolutely marvelous place. Incomparable wildlife. But it's not protected. Most of it is enormous ranches, private properties." While a national park exists here, it's not adequately patrolled. Warns Terborgh, "The world is adding 90 million people every year. They'll want to eat rice. Where will they grow it? The wetlands. They'll take the Pantanal and drain it, ditch it, convert it. It'll be one great rice paddy."

What's needed, he feels, is a whole new reserve, "designed so that the uppermost headwaters are protected. If you put it downstream, you're going to lose it for sure. That was the problem with Florida's Everglades— it's a downstream park, and now its bird populations are off 95 percent."

Consider one more South American reserve: Ecuador's Galápagos Islands National Park. In addition to its namesake tortoises (*galápagos* in Spanish), it boasts both terrestrial and marine iguanas, and 58 resident bird species. Of these, 28—including the flightless cormorant and the wonderfully diversified finches made famous by Darwin—are found nowhere else. Galápagos is not just a place, but also a metaphor for the crosscurrents between human and natural histories. Isolated for eons, wildlife here developed neither fear of humans nor effective defenses against exotic species. Sailors took hundreds of thousands of tortoises as fresh provender on long sea voyages. Settlers brought pigs, dogs, cats, and rats, all of which ravaged tortoise eggs and young, while introduced goats competed with adult tortoises for graze. In time, however, Ecuador declared this rocky archipelago a park and set up protective laws. Eradication attempts brought exotics under some measure of control, and in 1986 surrounding waters became a marine resource reserve. Today, Galápagos National Park may not be perfect, but it is a success.

So it is with other South American reserves. Many were degraded before earning protected status, and some continue to suffer from humans even now. Will the growing ecotourism industry become the salvation of these areas by guaranteeing them a solid economic base—or will it increase degradation by attracting too many visitors, too quickly? Opinions vary, especially with the particular refuge involved. Yet it seems clear that parks and other reserves are not a solution by themselves, not in South America or anywhere else. They are only a beginning. And while they remain the last, best hope for much of the world's wildlife, their ultimate success or failure is up to us.

Galápagos

Signature species of a strange archipelago, a male Galápagos tortoise mounts a smaller female. Centuries of human abuse decimated many creatures unique to these islands; Ecuador established the national park in 1959. FOLLOWING PAGES: Only seagoing lizards on earth, marine iguanas find refuge in offshore waters, part of Galápagos Marine Resource Reserve.

South America

Hato Piñero

Rare spectacled caimans (bottom, right) help draw visitors to Hato Piñero in Venezuela. Local attractions include the world's loudest small mammal, the red howler monkey, and the largest rodent, the capybara. Both cattle ranch and wildlife reserve, privately owned Hato Piñero finds tourist dollars in conservation. It boasts more than 300 bird species and a variety of other wildlife amid its mix of plateau, wetland, and gallery forest.

South America

Das Emas

In what some consider Brazil's finest national park, a giant anteater ransacks one of innumerable termite mounds that stud the area's dry, open grasslands. Das Emas translates from the Portuguese as "of the rheas," which reflects the prevalence of the park's fauna. Rheas, flightless birds similar to ostriches, race throughout the park, as do armadillos (opposite).

Patagonia (Overleaf) ▷

Wild as their realm, guanacos greet the sunrise in southern Chile's spectacular Torres del Paine National Park. Other Patagonian sanctuaries include Argentina's Perito Moreno, Los Glaciares, and Tierra del Fuego.

South America

Notes on Contributors

London-born and Oxford-educated, **Douglas Botting** is the author of several travel books, including *Wilderness Europe*, *Rio de Janeiro*, and *One Chilly Siberian Morning*. In addition, he has made many television documentaries. A fellow of the Royal Geographical Society, he has traveled extensively.

Born of American parents in Beirut, Lebanon, **Patrick R. Booz** grew up in Pakistan and Indonesia and earned a degree in Asian studies at the University of Wisconsin. The author of the China chapter in the Special Publication *Beyond the Horizon*, he combines his writing skills with fluency in three Chinese dialects.

Kenneth Brower authored the Special Publication *Yosemite* and has written several other volumes, including *The Starship and the Canoe*, that chronicle a lifelong interest in wilderness, nature, and ecology. His books and articles in NATIONAL GEOGRAPHIC, National Geographic TRAVELER, and other magazines have taken him throughout North America and around the world.

A member of the Society staff since 1971, senior writer **Tom Melham** concentrates on outdoor adventure and environmental themes, principally in Alaska and South America. In addition to contributing numerous chapters to Special Publications, he has authored *Alaska's Wildlife Treasures* and *John Muir's Wild America*, and has co-authored *Alaska's Magnificent Parklands*.

Graham Pizzey, author of *A Separate Creation: Discovery of Wild Australia* and several other books, has been photographing and writing about Australia's birds and other animals for decades. For nearly 20 years he contributed a weekly article to the Melbourne *Herald*. Active in conservation, he was made a member of the Order of Australia for his services to ornithology.

A trained zoologist and a scientific fellow of the Zoological Society, **Anthony Smith** is the author of more than 20 books, many of which focus on Africa. Based in London, he has visited Africa many times and returns as often as he can. He studied zoology at Oxford and remains a keen naturalist and inveterate traveler.

Acknowledgments

The Book Division wishes to thank the individuals, groups, and organizations named or quoted in the text for their help in the preparation of this volume. In addition, we are grateful for the assistance of the following: Daniel Blanco, Asociación de Conservación para la Selva Sur; Nick Bowles; Mark Bretzfelder, National Zoological Park; Pat Buechner, Embassy of Australia; Stacy Churchwell and Terry McEneaney, Yellowstone National Park; Phillippa Cobley; Charles Crumly; Adolfo Cuentas; Lu Ann Dietz, Chng Soh Koon, World Wildlife Fund International; Louise Emmons, Mark Epstein, Robert Fadden, Mercedes Foster, Robert Gordon, Roy McDiarmid, David Nickle, Mike Pogue, Bob Reynolds, Smithsonian Institution; Ted Hollis; Carlos Llanos; Boris Gomez Luna; Christopher Mead, British Trust for Ornithology; Greg Miles, Kakadu National Park; Carol Mitchell; Larkspur Morton; Jonelle Nuckolls; Roger Pasquier; Kent Redford; Royal Society for the Protection of Birds; Paul Sheller; Amy Vedder, Wildlife Conservation Society; and Walter Wust.

Additional Reading

Readers may wish to consult the *National Geographic Index* for related articles. The following may also be useful: Douglas Botting, *Wilderness Europe*; Stanley Breeden and Belinda Wright, *Kakadu: Looking After the Country—The Gagudju Way*; Richard Burton, ed., *Nature's Last Strongholds*; Douglas Chadwick, *The Fate of the Elephant*; Kai Curry-Lindahl, *Europe—A Natural History*; Roger Few, *The Atlas of Wild Places*; Max Finlayson and Michael Moser, *Wetlands*; Adrian Forsyth, *Portraits of the Rain Forest*; Seymour L. Fishbein, *Yellowstone Country*; Frans Lanting and Christine K. Eckstrom, *Forgotten Edens: Exploring the World's Wild Places*; William Leitch, *South America's National Parks*; Kim McQuarrie and Andre and Cornelia Bartschi, *Peru's Amazonian Eden: Manu National Park and Biosphere Reserve*; George Schaller, *The Last Panda*; Anthony Smith, *The Great Rift*; G. Causey Whittow, *Malaysian Wildlife*; World Conservation Monitering Centre, *1993 United Nations List of National Parks and Protected Areas*.

Index

Boldface indicates illustrations.

Spines for the spiny: A land iguana in Ecuador's legendary Galápagos Islands sanctuary gnaws a pad of prickly pear cactus.

Less than two feet high at the shoulder, an agile, chamois-like klipspringer stands guard over the boulder-studded veld of South Africa's Karoo National Park.

Blue-winged kookaburra—a ground-hunting cousin of the European kingfisher—downs a lizard in Australia's Kakadu National Park, in the continent's wild Northern Territory.

Illustrations Credits

Cover: Daniel. J. Cox. **Front Matter:** 1 Anthony Bannister/NHPA. 2-3 Graham Robertson/Auscape. 4-5 Planet Earth Pictures/K&K Ammann. 6-7 Robert C. Nunnington/ABPL. 8-9 Anthony Bannister/NHPA. **Chapter 1 - Africa:** 10-11 Robert Caputo/Aurora. 12 Grant Dixon/Australasian Nature Transparencies. 13 Frans Lanting. 16-17 Mark Deeble and Victoria Stone. 18 Art Wolfe. 18-19 Ferrero/Labat/Auscape. 20-21 Günter Ziesler. 22-23 Günter Ziesler. 23 Rich Kirchner. 24-25 Planet Earth Pictures/Jonathan Scott. 26-27 Ferrero/Labat/Auscape. 27 (left), Stan Osolinski/Oxford Scientific Films; (right), Joe McDonald. 28-29 Ferrero/Labat/Auscape. 31 Louise Gubb/J.B. Pictures. 34 Klaus Paysan. 37 Frans Lanting. 38-39 James Carmichael, Jr./NHPA. 40 Frans Lanting. 40-41 Martin Harvey/Australasian Nature Transparencies. 41 Martin Harvey/Natural Science Photos. 42-43 (both), Michael Nichols/Magnum. 44 Janos Jurka/NaturFotograferna/N. 44-45, 45 Nigel Dennis/ABPL. 46, 47 Martin Harvey/Australasian Nature Transparencies. **Chapter 2 - Europe:** Hellio & Van Ingen/NHPA. 50 Planet Earth Pictures/John Eastcott & Yva Momatiuk. 51 Michael Leach/Oxford Scientific Films. 54, 54-55 Jan Töve/Planet Earth Pictures. 55 Robert Maier/Aquila Photographics. 56-57 Hellio & Van Ingen/NHPA. 58 Incafo/Antonio Camoyan. 58-59 Henry Ausloos/NHPA. 67 Günter Ziesler. 68 (upper), Günter Ziesler; (lower), Robert Maier/Aquila Photographics. 69 Mark Hamblin/Oxford Scientific Films. 70-71 Raymond Gehman. 72 Riccardo Villarosa/Overseas/Oxford Scientific Films. 73 B. & C. Alexander. 74-75 Janos Jurka/Bruce Coleman, LTD. **Chapter 3 - Asia:** 76-77 E. & D. Hosking/FLPA. 78 Robert & Linda Mitchell. 79 Frans Lanting/Minden Pictures. 82 Gerald Cubitt/Bruce Coleman, LTD. 82-83 Martin Harvey/NHPA. 84-85 Raghu Rai/Magnum. 86 Jean-Pierre Zwaenepoel/Bruce Coleman, LTD. 86-87 Martin Harvey/NHPA. 88 Raghu Rai/Magnum. 90 Bradley H. Simpson. 93 Raghu Rai/Magnum. 95 Konrad Wothe. 96 (upper, middle, lower), Robert & Linda Mitchell. 96-97 Michael Fogden/DRK Photo. 98, 99 Jean-Paul Ferrero/Auscape. 100-101, 101 George B. Schaller. 102-103 Teiji Saga/Tony Stone Images. 104-105 Natalie B. Fobes/Tony Stone Images. 105 Jacana/Yves Lanceau. **Chapter 4 - Australia:** 106-107 David Doubilet. 108 J. & E.S. Baker/Australasian Nature Transparencies. 109 Steve Turner/Oxford Scientific Films. 112 (upper), Jean-Paul Ferrero/Auscape; (lower), D. & V. Blagden/Australasian Nature Transparencies. 112-113 Brendan Beirne/Auscape. 114-115 Peter Cook/Auscape. 116 Dr. Dawn W. Frith/Bruce Coleman, Inc. 117 Ralph & Daphne Keller/Australasian Nature Transparencies. 118-119 Martin Harvey/Natural Science Photos. 120 John Canin/Australasian Nature Transparencies. 126 Dave Watts/Australasian Nature Transparencies. 126-127 Ted Mead/Australasian Nature Transparencies. 127 Dave Watts/Australasian Nature Transparencies. 128, 128-129 David Doubilet. 129 Alby Ziebell/Auscape. 130 B.G. Thomson/Australasian Nature Transparencies. 130-131 J. Frazier/Australasian Nature Transparencies. 132-133 Otto Rogge/NHPA. **Chapter 5 - North America:** 134-135 Animals Animals/Marty Stouffer. 136 Linde Waidhofer. 137 Daniel J. Cox/Tony Stone Images. 140-141 Rich Kirchner. 142-143 Joe McDonald. 143 Rich Kirchner. 144 Linde Waidhofer. 144-145 Alan & Sandy Carey. 145 Rich Kirchner. 146 Daniel J. Cox. 153 Joe McDonald. 154-155, 155 Daniel J. Cox. 156 (upper), Planet Earth Pictures/Brian Kenney; (lower), Chris Johns. 156-157 Chris Johns. 158-159 Ron Sanford. 160-161 (upper), Carol Farneti Fosax/Natural Science Photos; (lower), Michael & Patricia Fogden. 161 Jim Clare/Partridge Films LTD/Oxford Scientific Films. 162-163, 163 Joe McDonald. 164 Tom & Pat Leeson. 165 Skip Moody/Dembinsky Photo Associates. 166-167 Tom Ulrich/Oxford Scientific Films. **Chapter 6 - South America:** 168-169 Tui De Roy/Auscape. 170 Will & Deni McIntyre/Tony Stone Images. 171 Günter Ziesler. 174-175 Planet Earth Pictures/André Bärtschi. 175 (upper), J. C. Munoz/Incafo; (lower), Planet Earth Pictures/André Bärtschi. 176-177 Martin Wendler/NHPA. 178 Jim Clare/Partridge Films Ltd/Oxford Scientific Films. 179 (upper), Warren Martin Hern; (lower), Günter Ziesler. 180 Frans Lanting/Minden Pictures. 187 Tui De Roy/Auscape. 188-189 Howard Hall/Oxford Scientific Films. 190 Planet Earth Pictures/André Bärtschi. 190-191, 191 Art Wolfe. 192 Haroldo Palo/NHPA. 192-193, 194-195 Günter Ziesler. **Back Matter:** 197 Wolfgang Kaehler. 198 Nigel Dennis/NHPA. 199 Joe McDonald.

Library of Congress CIP Data

Animal kingdoms : wildlife sanctuaries of the world / prepared by the
  Book Division, National Geographic Society.
      p.   cm.
    Includes index.
    ISBN 0-7922-2734-4
    1. Wildlife refuges. 2. National Parks and reserves. 3. Wildlife
  refuges—Pictorial works. 4. National parks and reserves—Pictorial
  works. I. National Geographic Society (U.S.). Book Division.
  QL82.A55 1995
  333.95'4—dc20   95-11922
                                                                         CIP

Composition for this book by the National Geographic Society Book Division with the assistance of the Typographic section of National Geographic Production Services, Pre-Press Division. Printed and bound by R. R. Donnelley & Sons, Willard, Ohio. Color separations by Digital Color Image, Cherry Hill, N.J.; Graphic Art Service, Inc., Nashville, Tenn.; Lanman Progressive Co., Washington, D.C.; Penn Colour Graphics, Inc., Huntingdon Valley, Pa.; and Phototype Color Graphics, Pennsauken, N.J. Dust jacket printed by Miken Systems, Inc., Cheektowaga, N.Y.